# HOW TO DRAW
# ANIMALS
## FOR KIDS

## THIS BOOK BELONGS TO :

........................................................

Your Opinion matters to us
Please do not hesitate to leave a comment
In the Amazon website.

# Pets

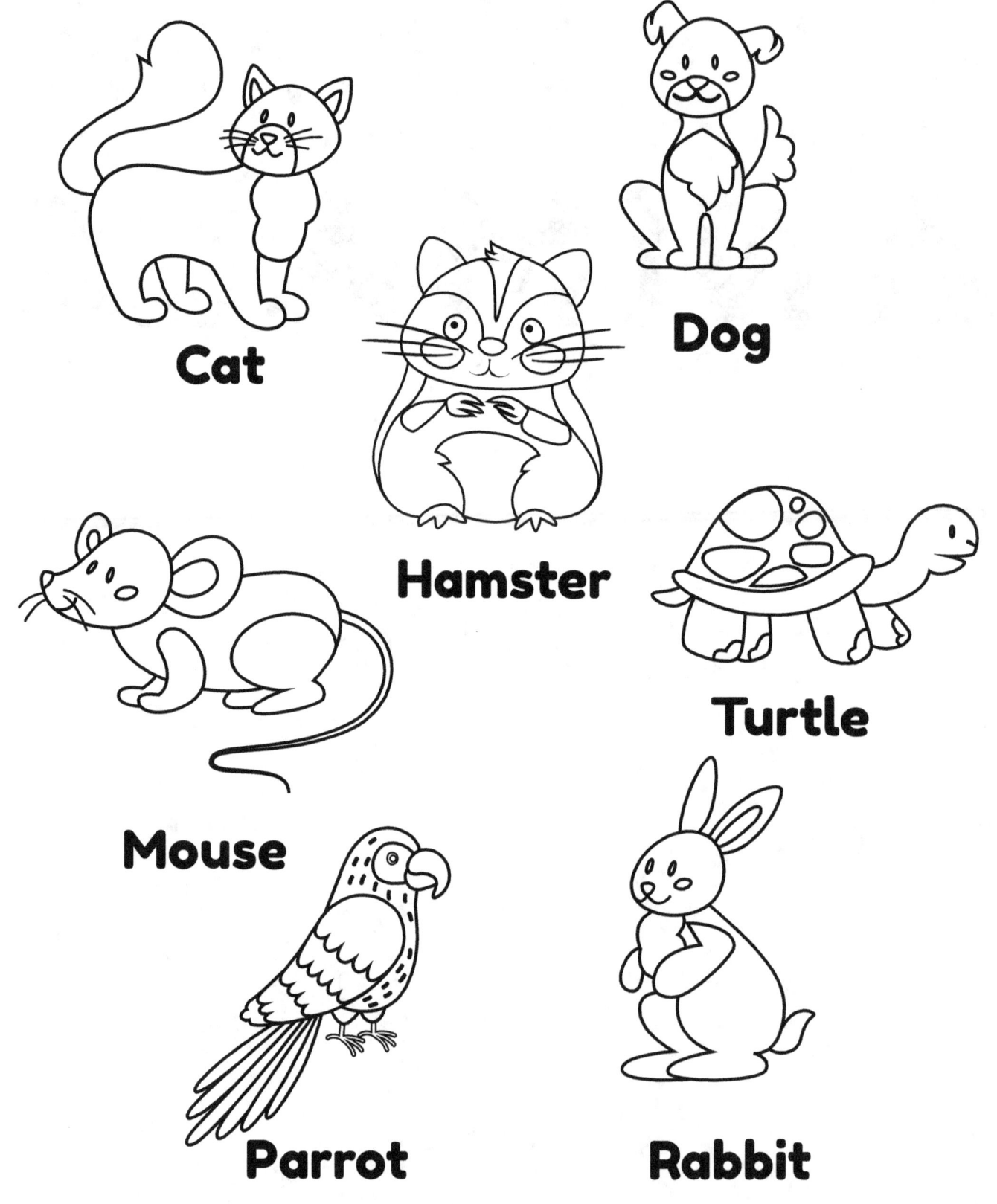

Cat

Dog

Hamster

Mouse

Turtle

Parrot

Rabbit

# Dog

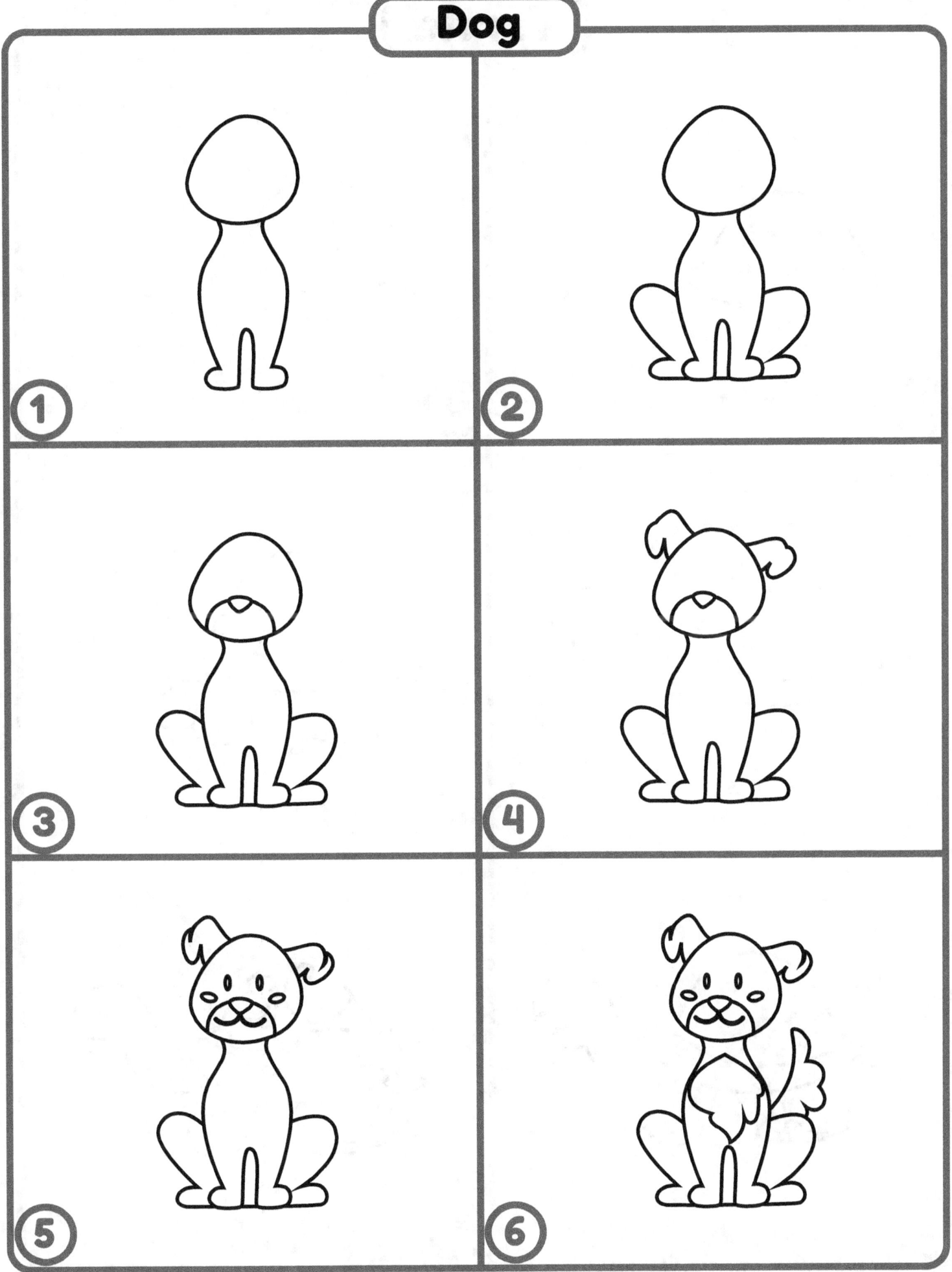

# Turtle

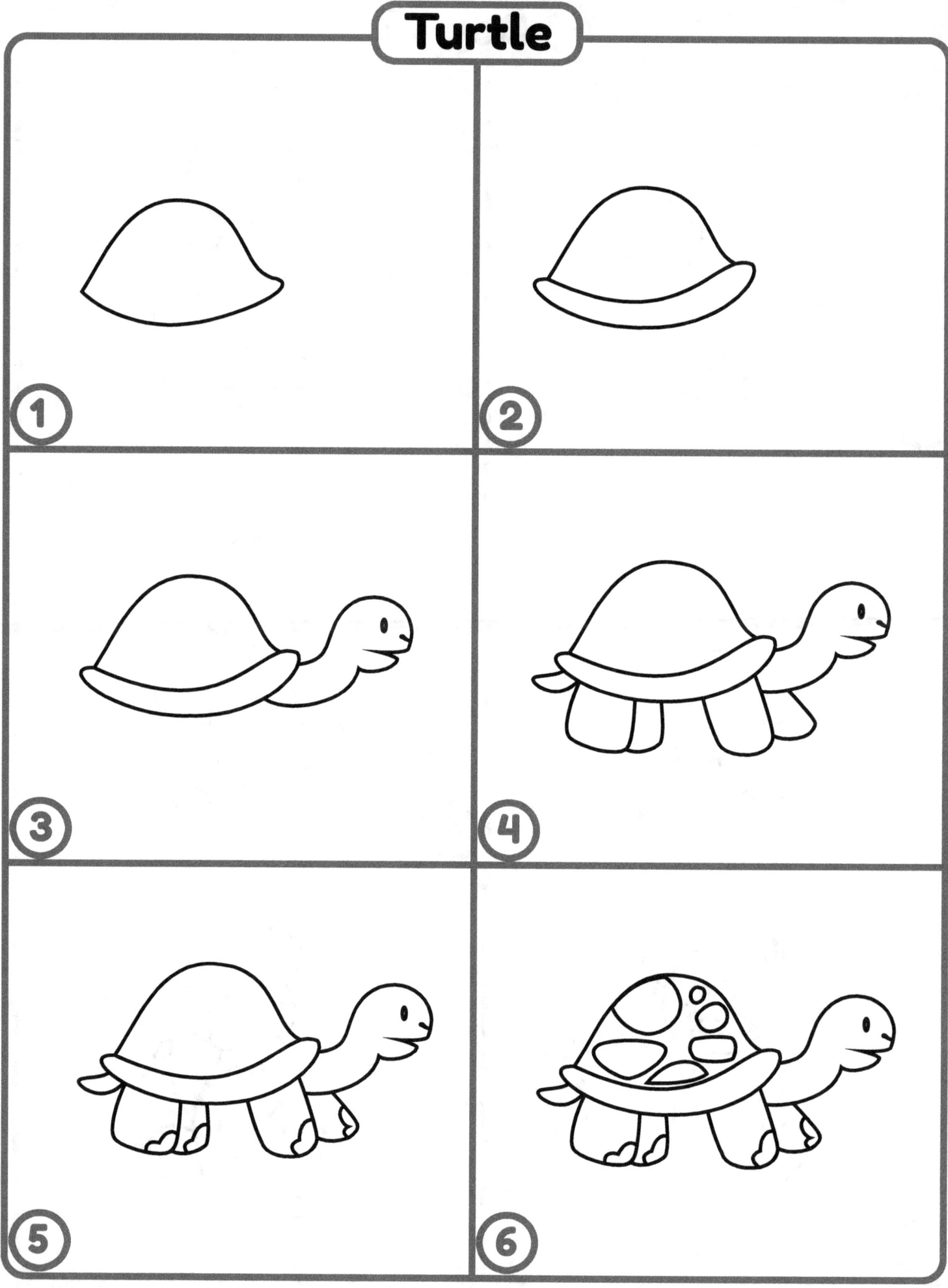

# Cat

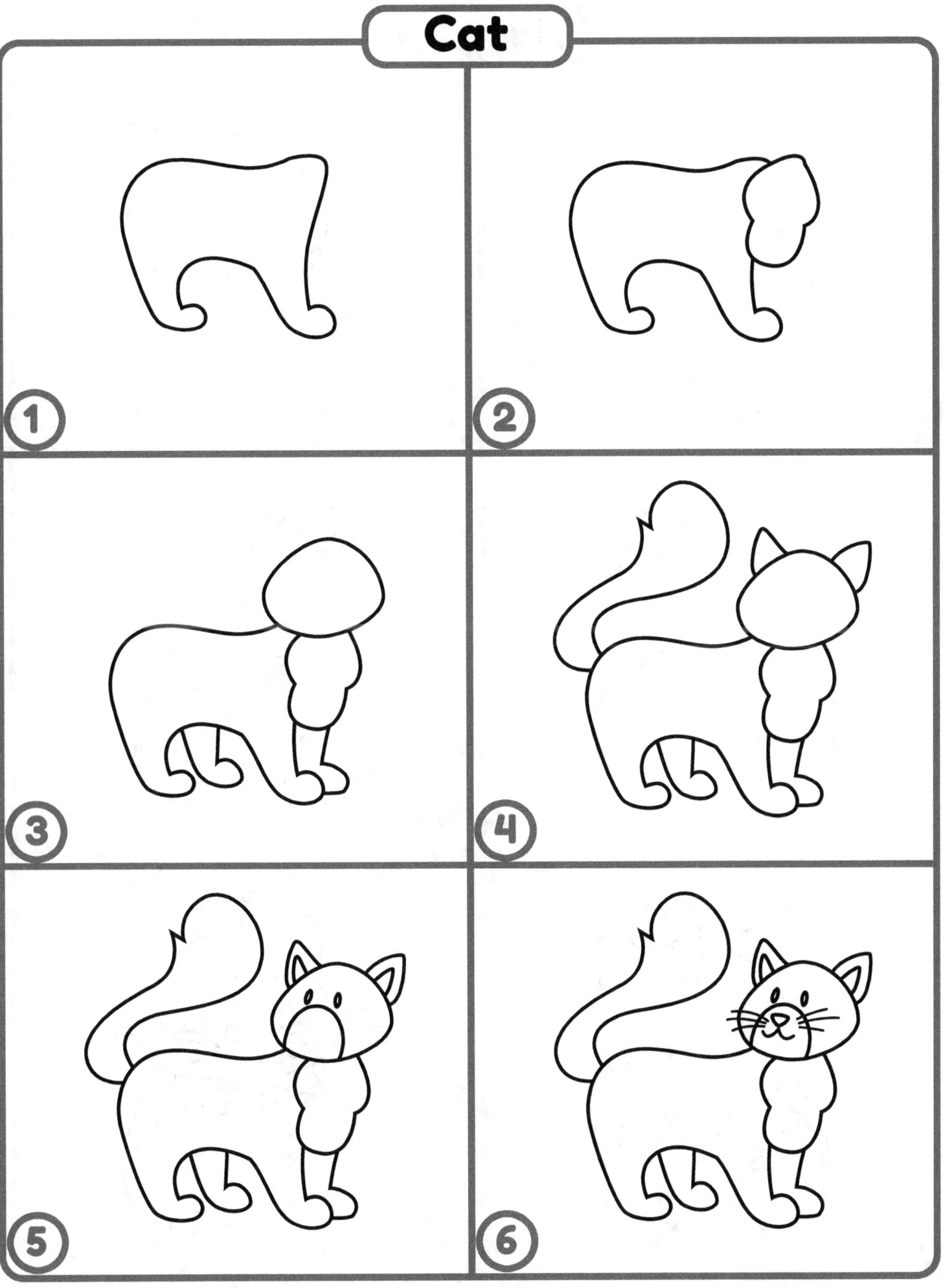

# Hamster

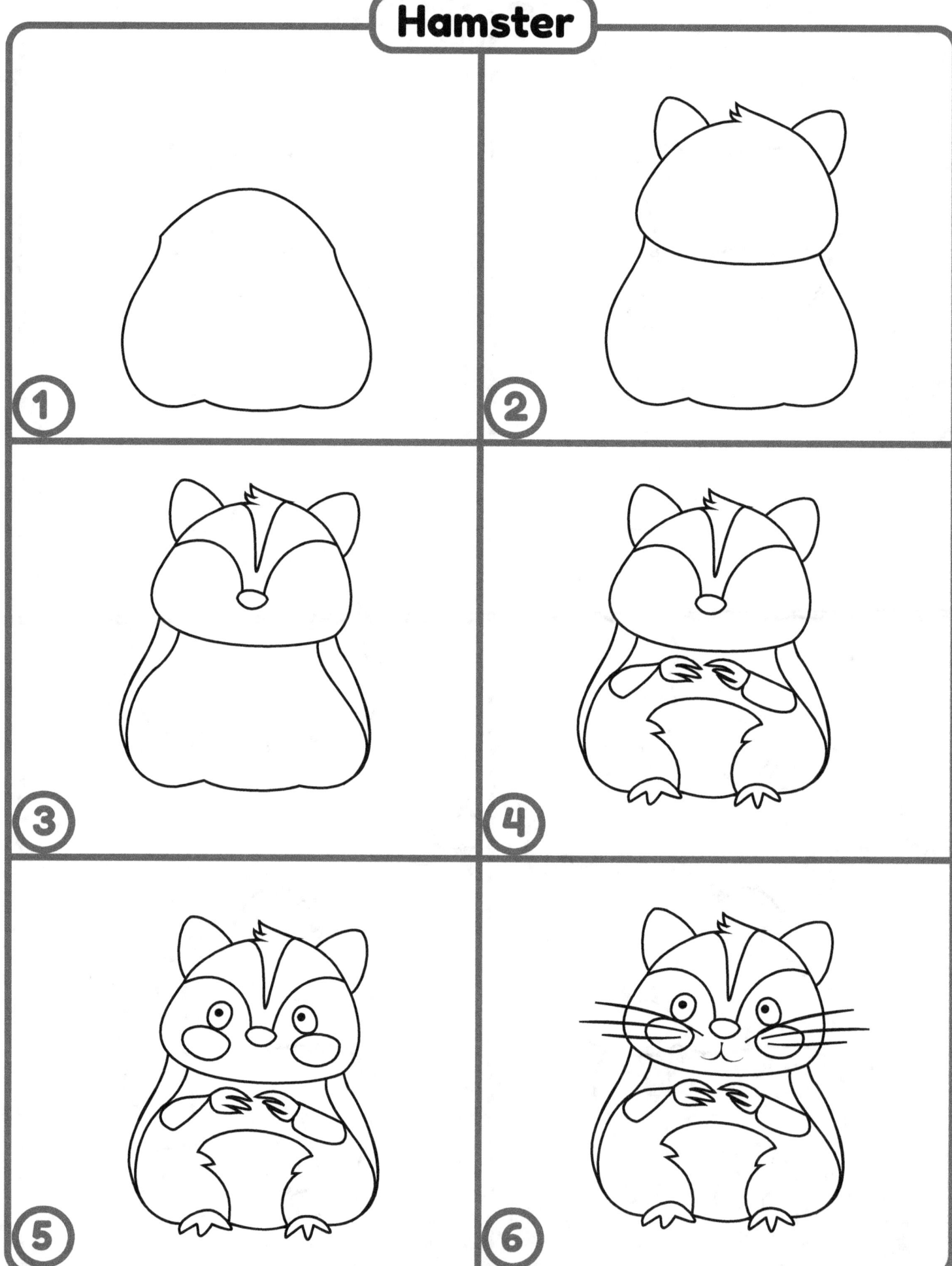

# Mouse

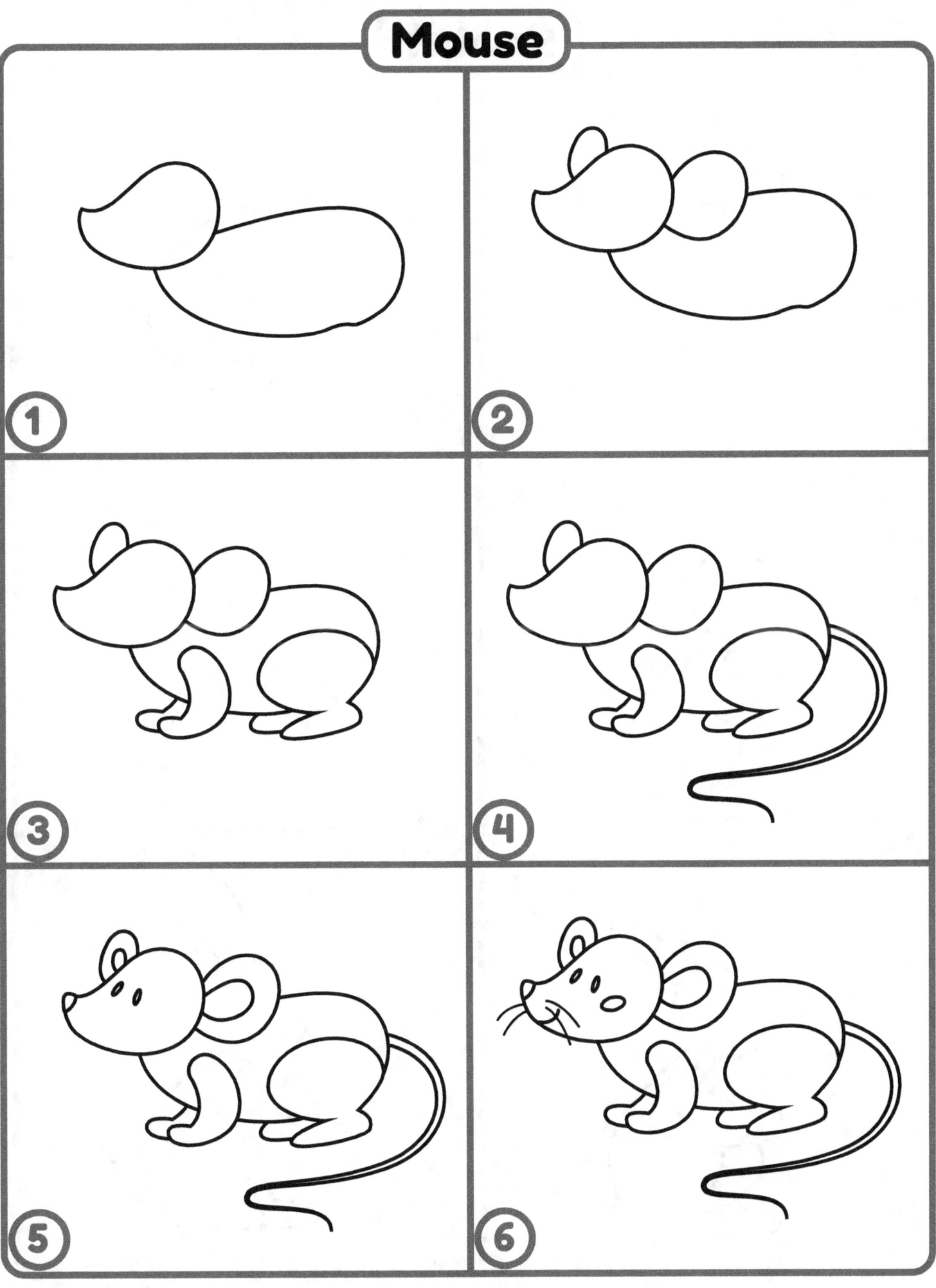

# Rabbit

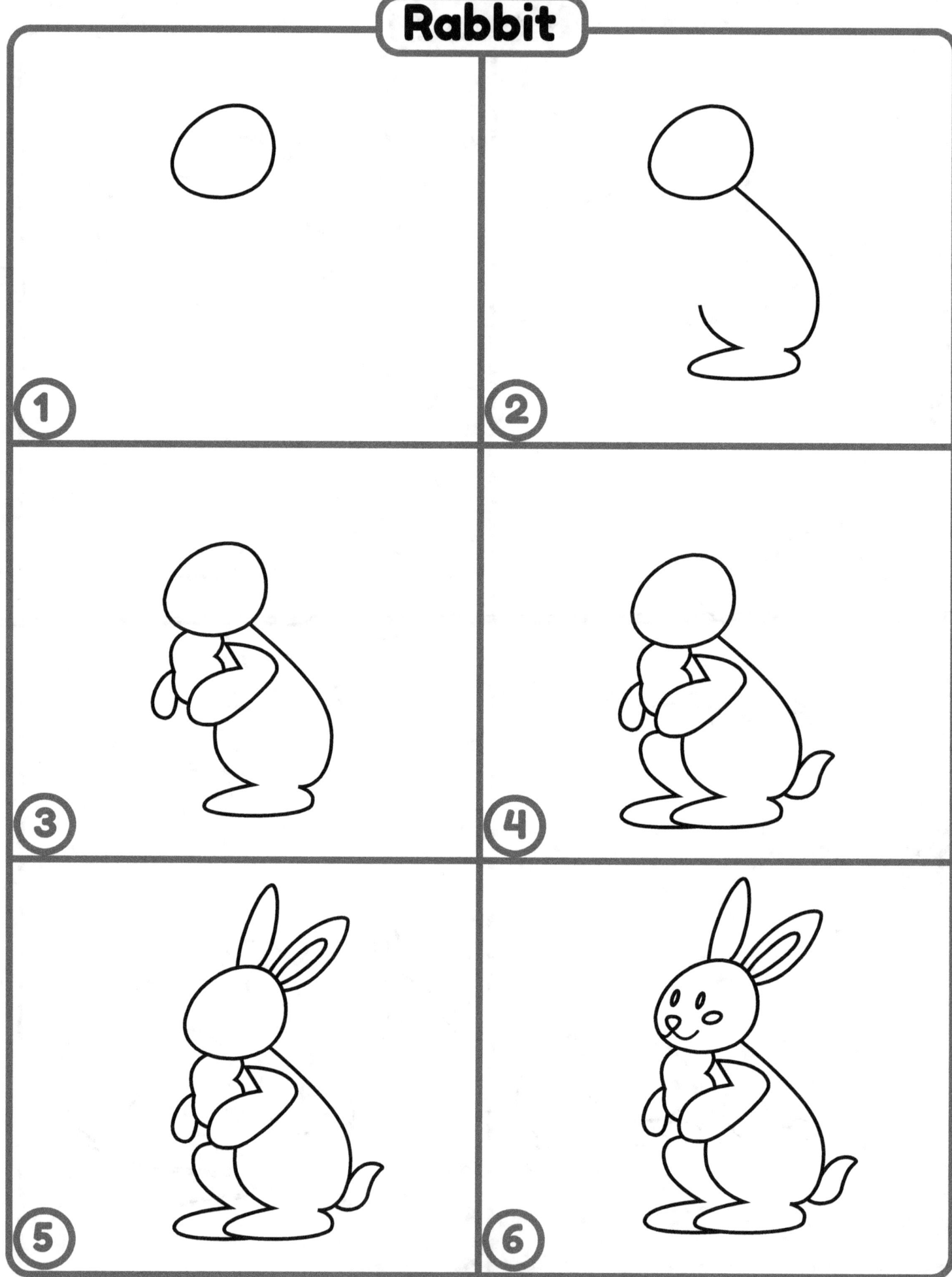

# Parrot

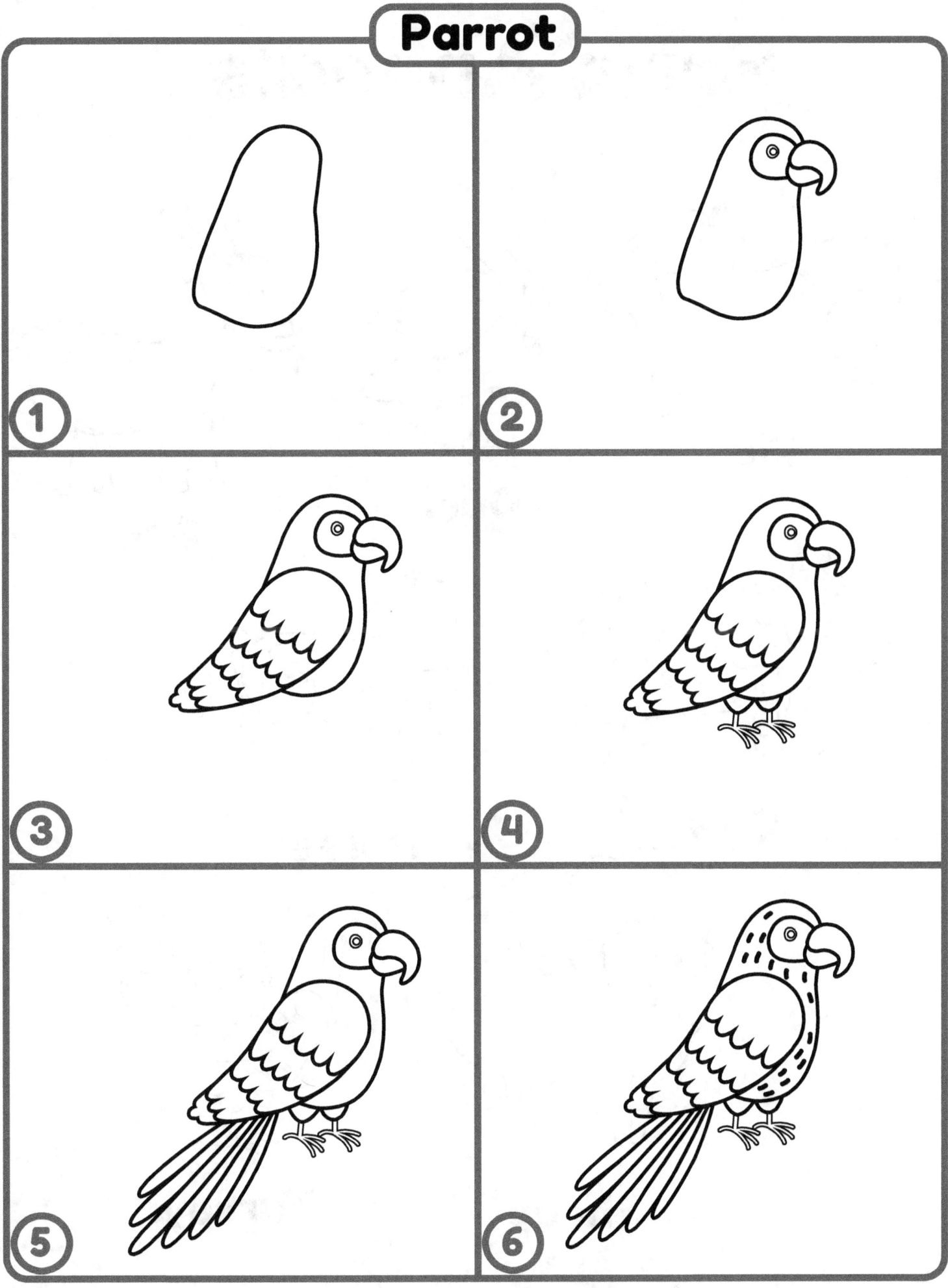

# Farm Animals

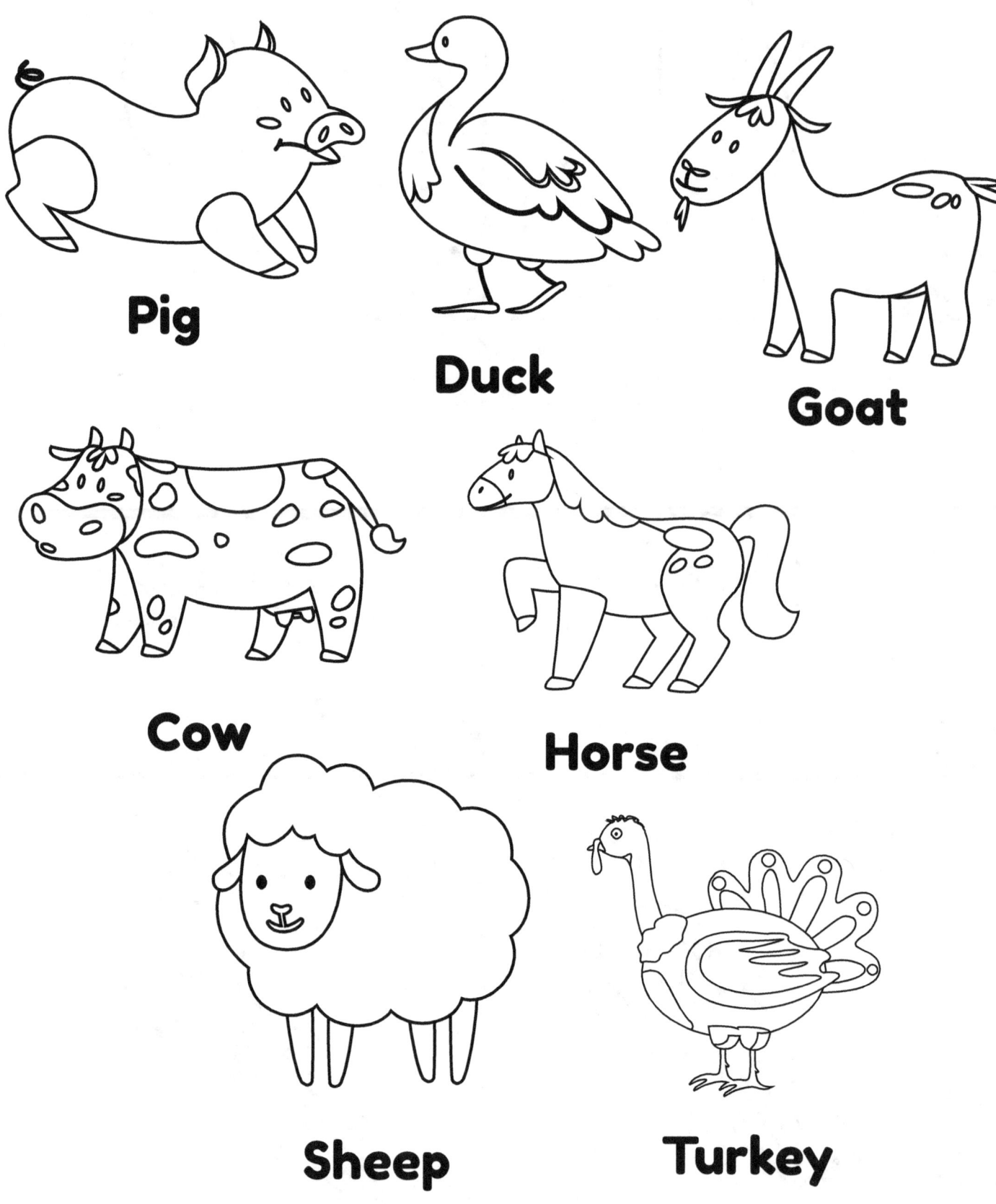

Pig

Duck

Goat

Cow

Horse

Sheep

Turkey

# Cow

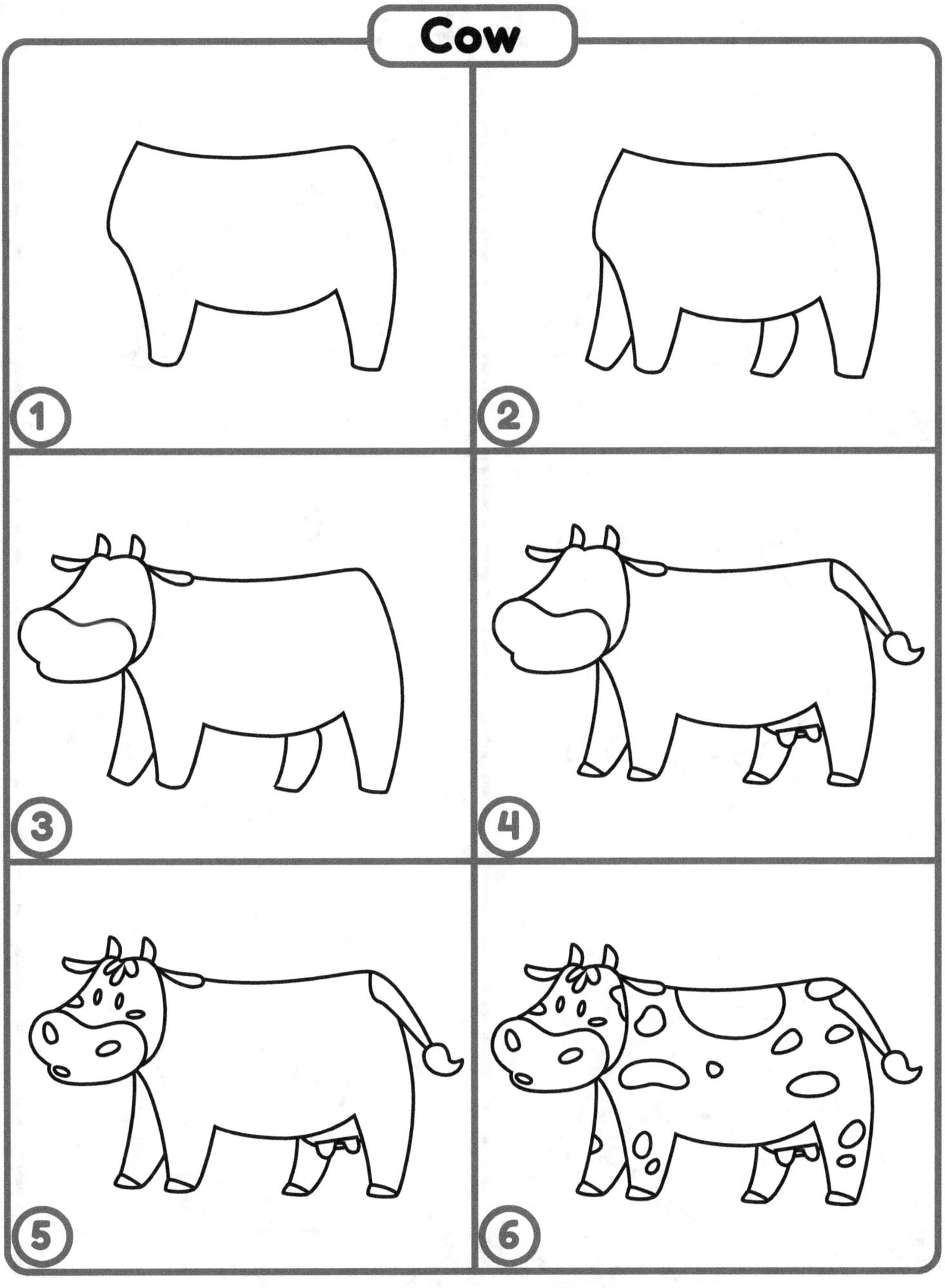

# Duck

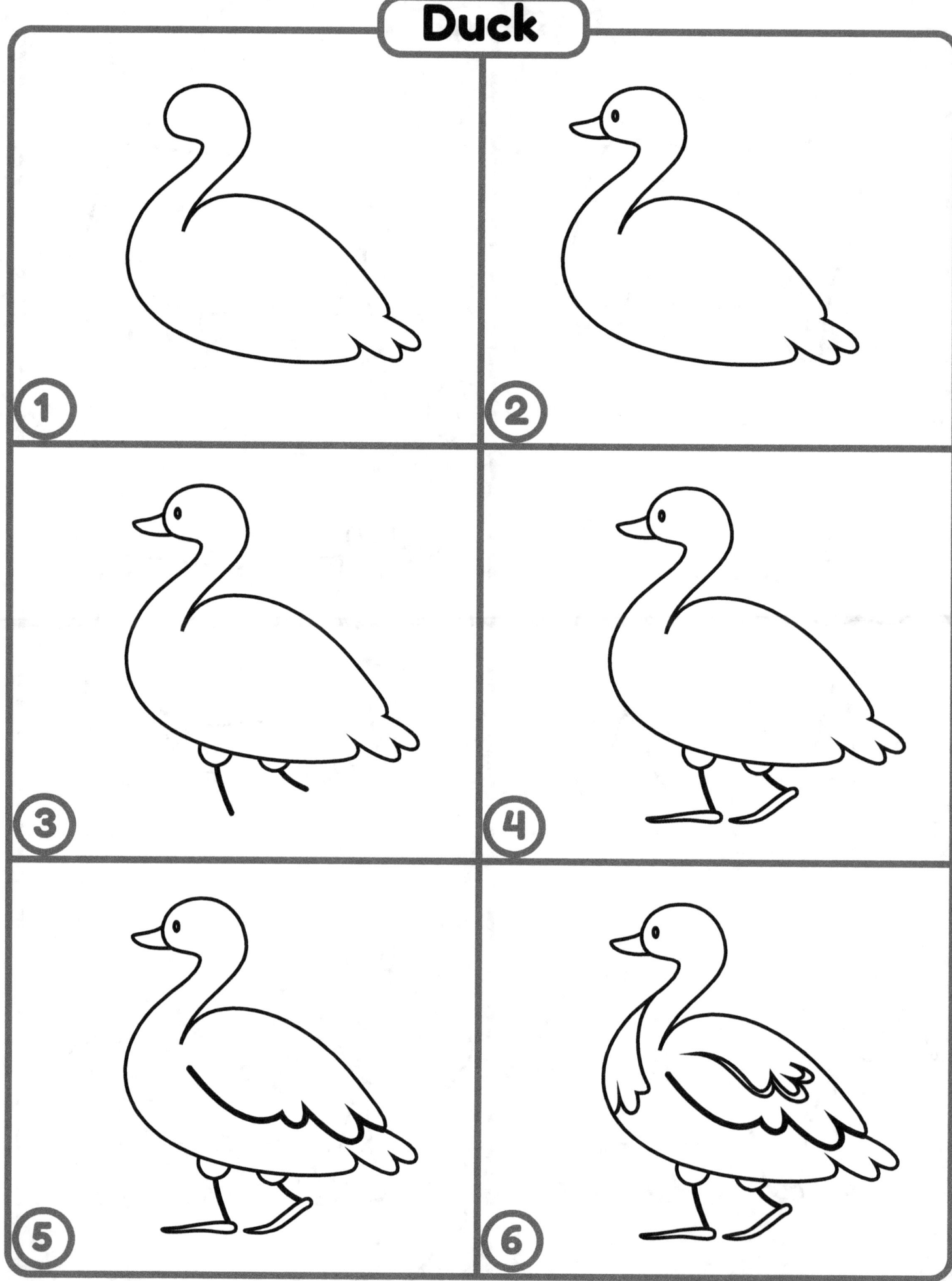

# Pig

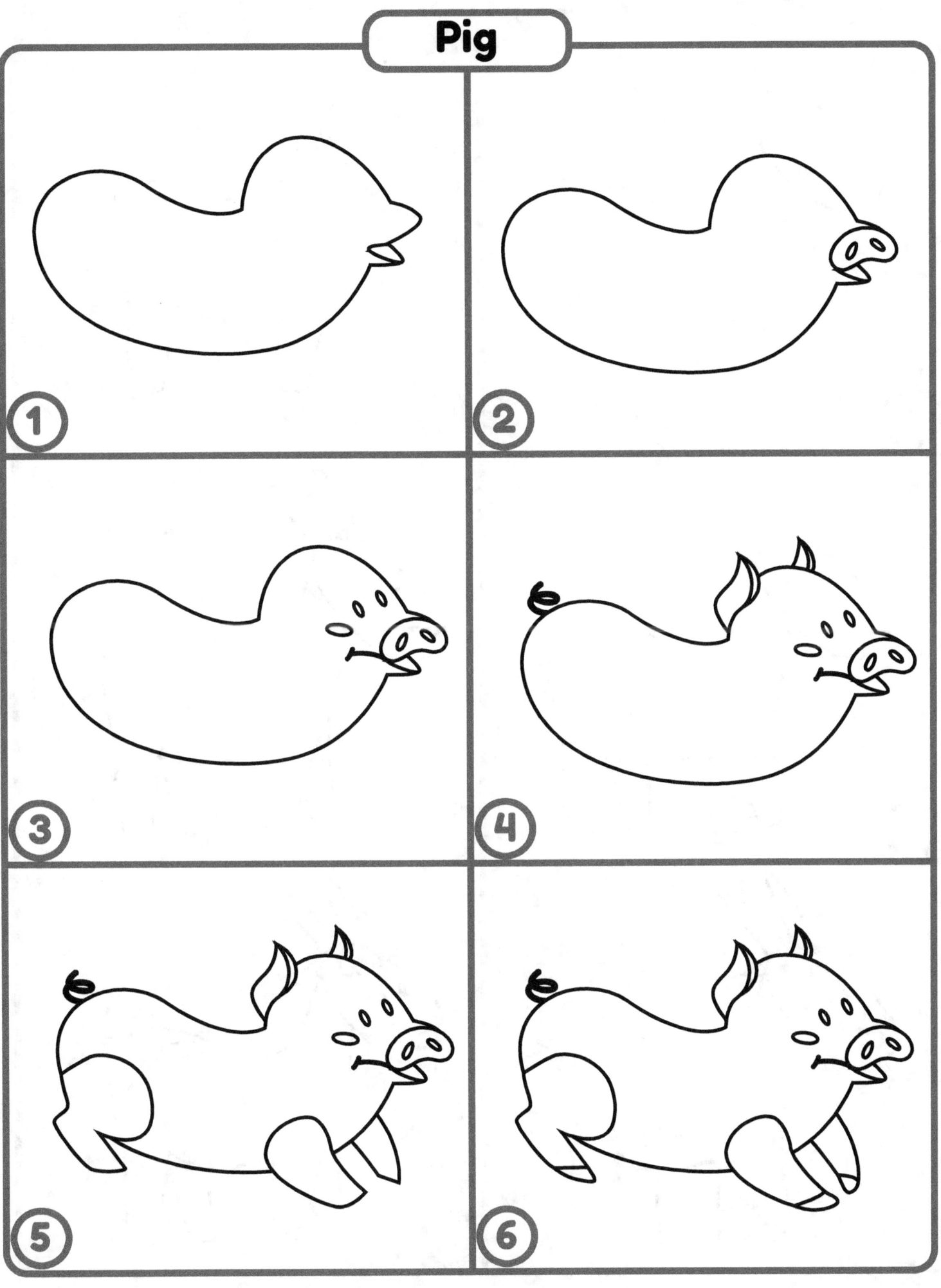

# Goat

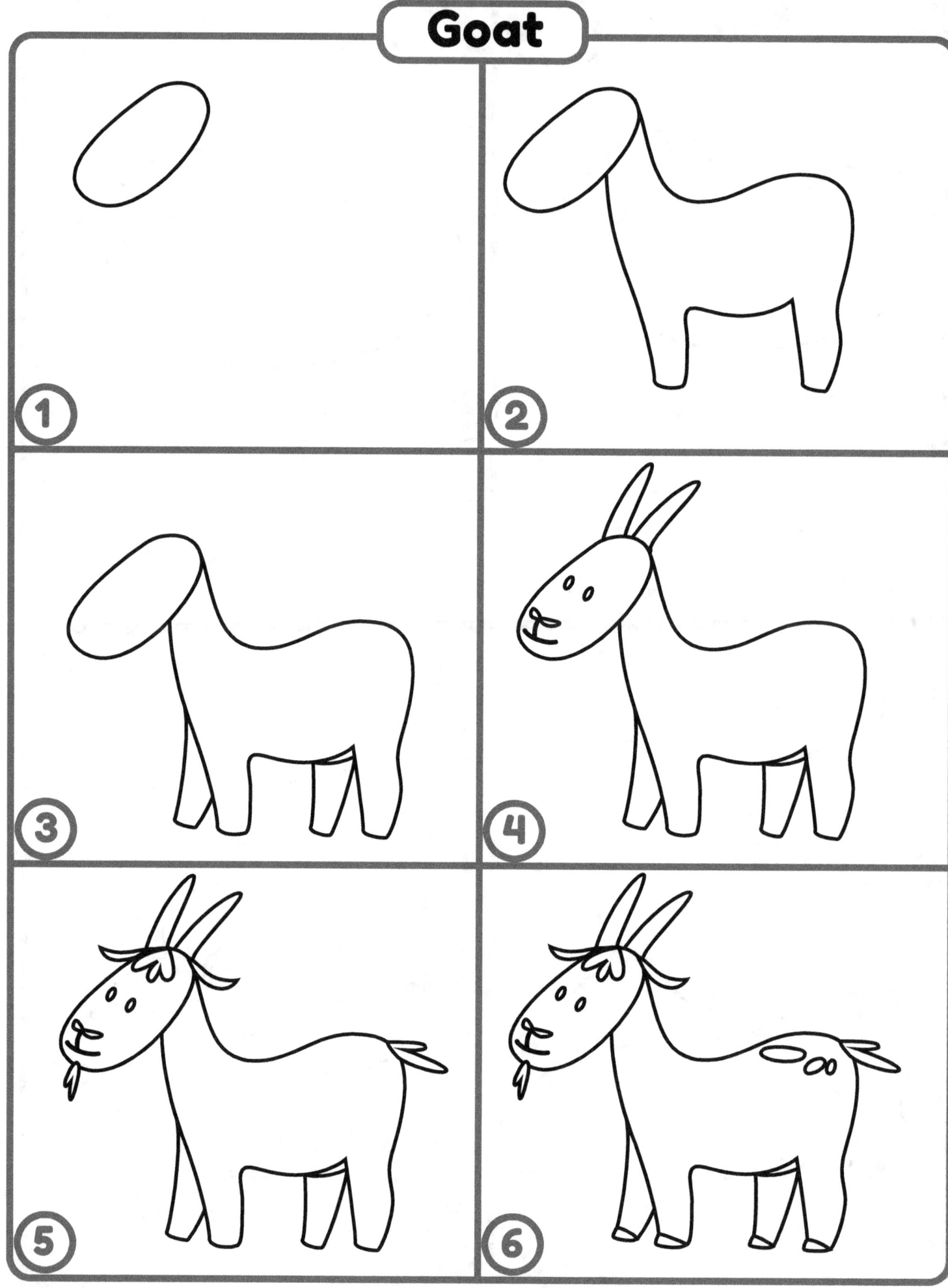

# Sheep

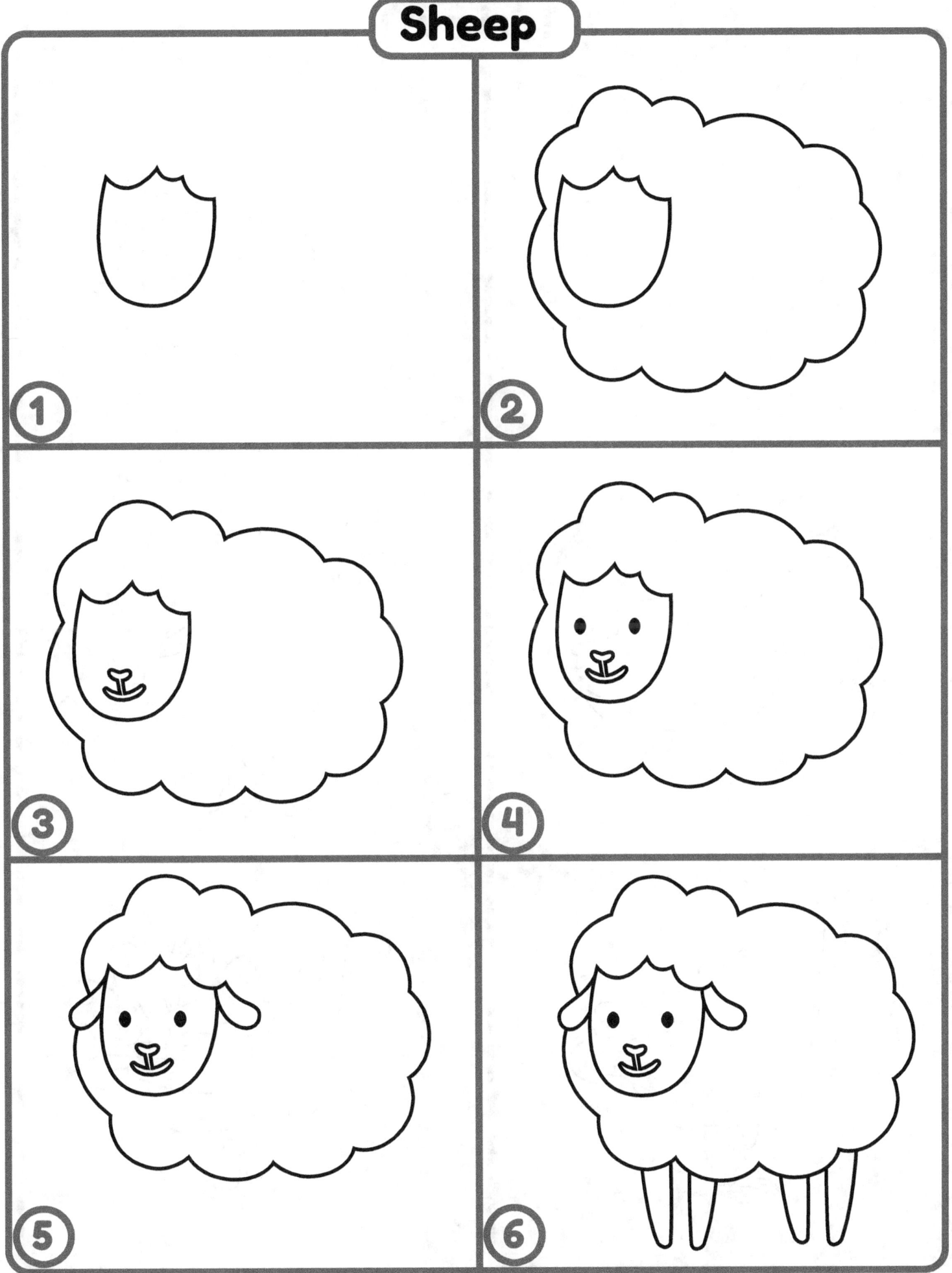

# Turkey

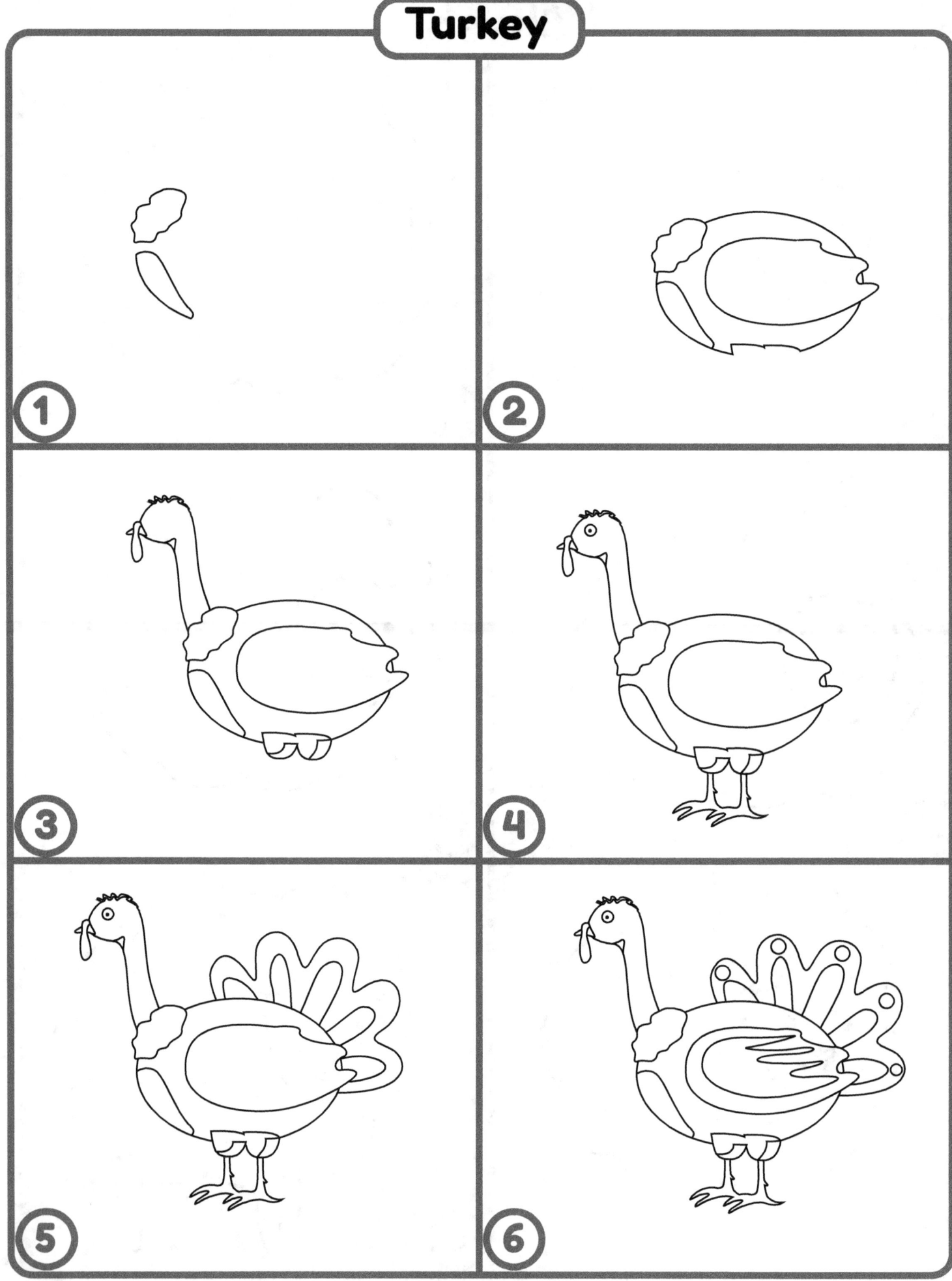

# Horse

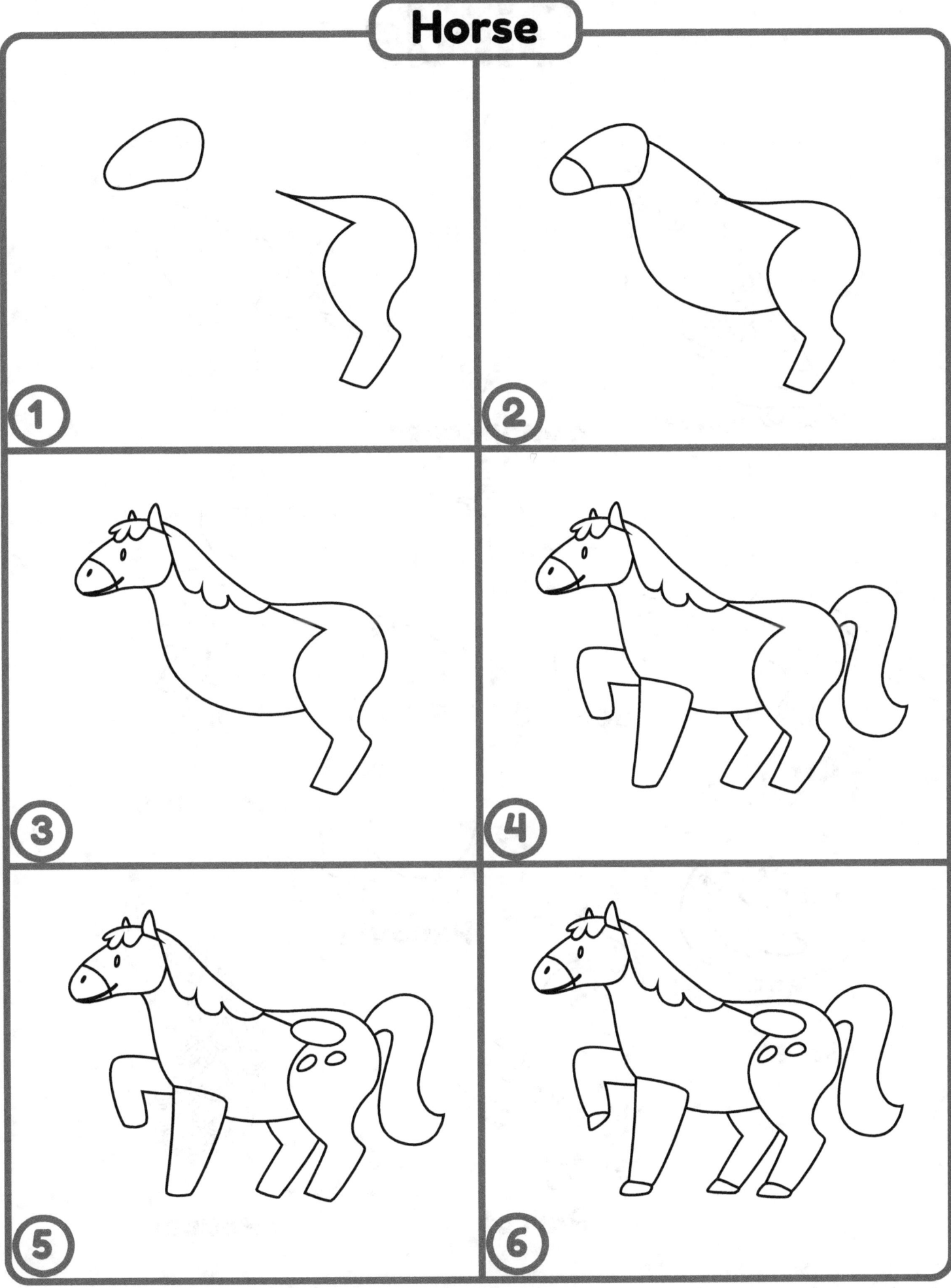

# Birds

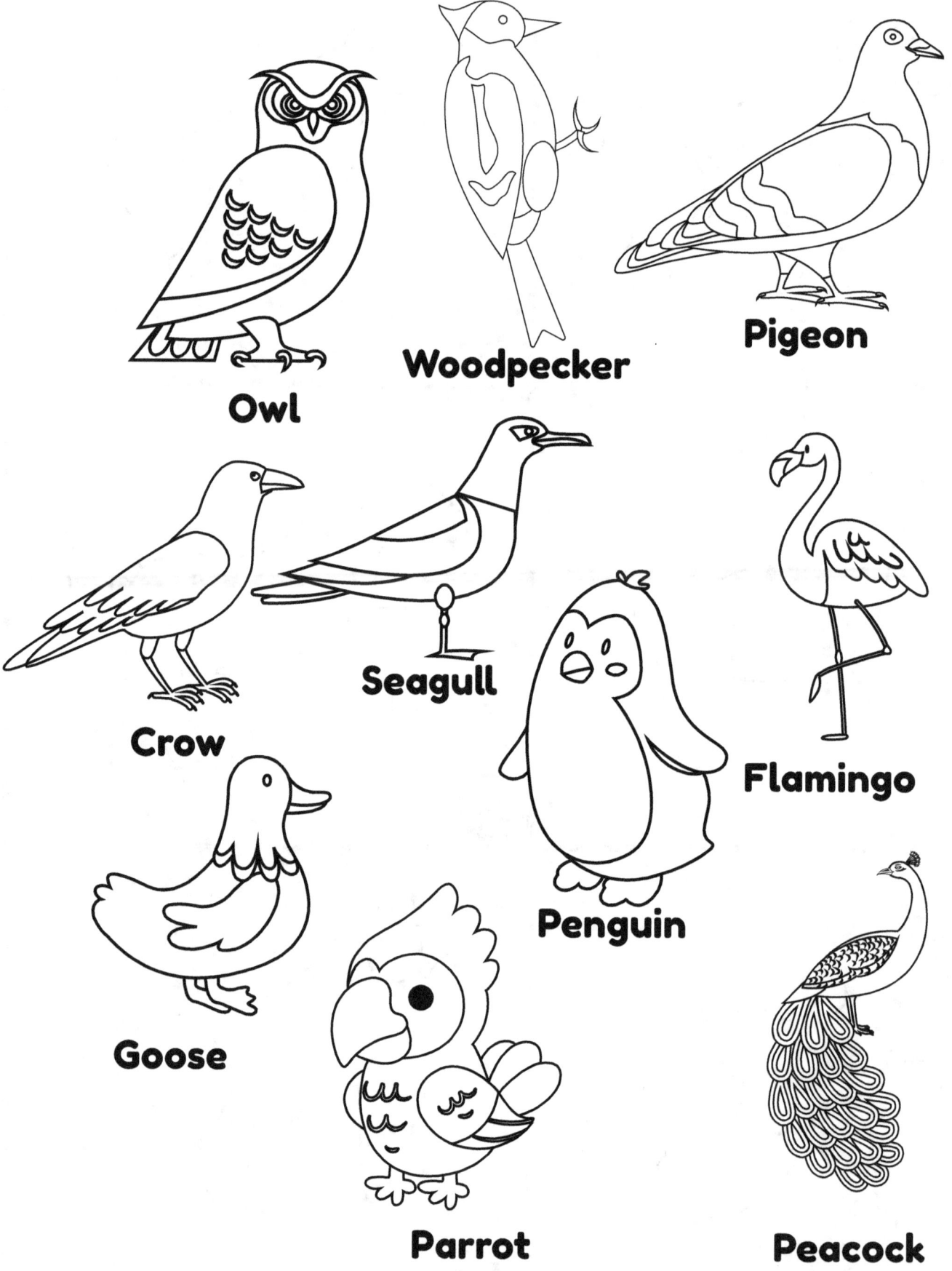

Owl

Woodpecker

Pigeon

Crow

Seagull

Penguin

Flamingo

Goose

Parrot

Peacock

# Peacock

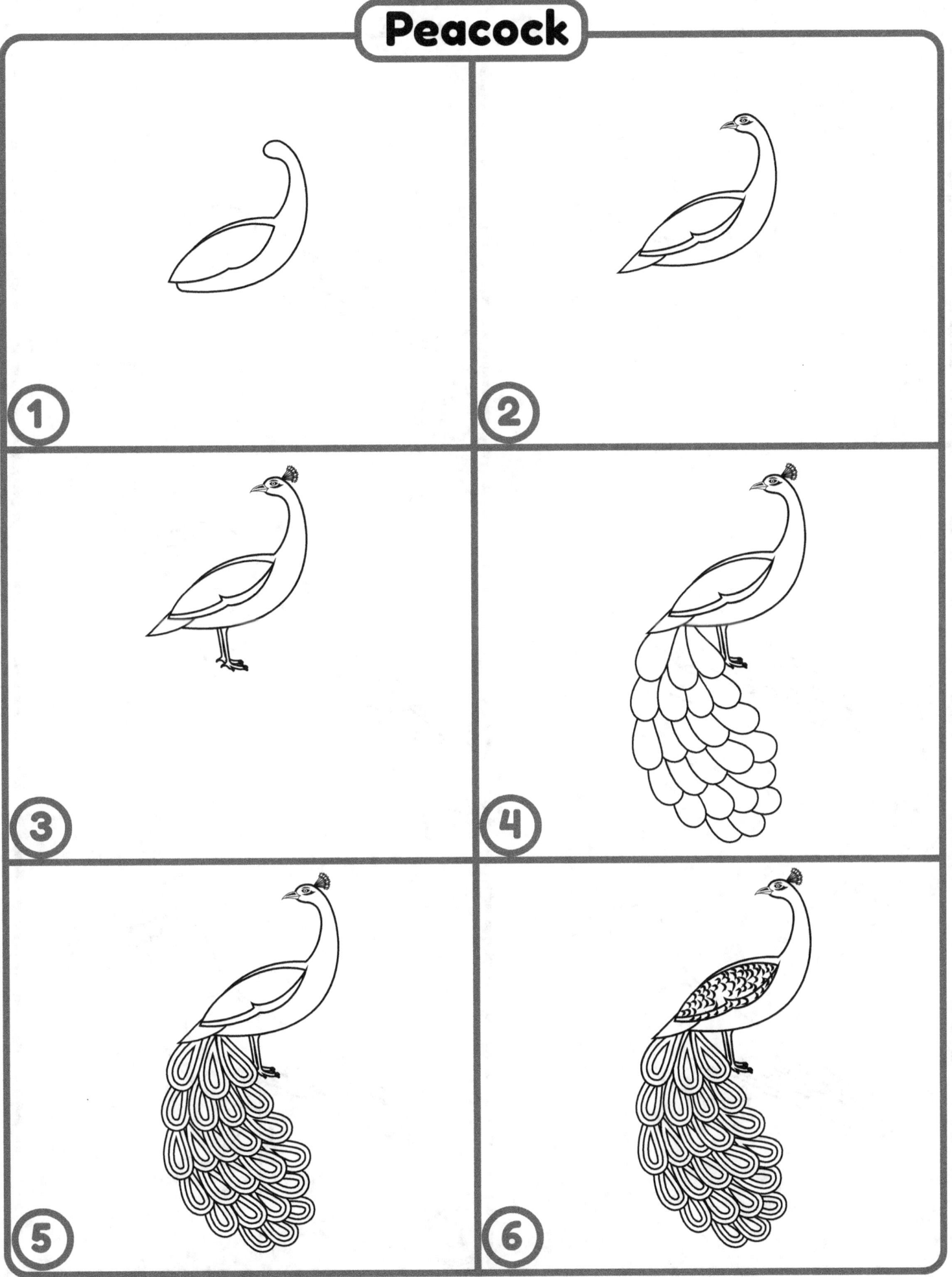

# Crow

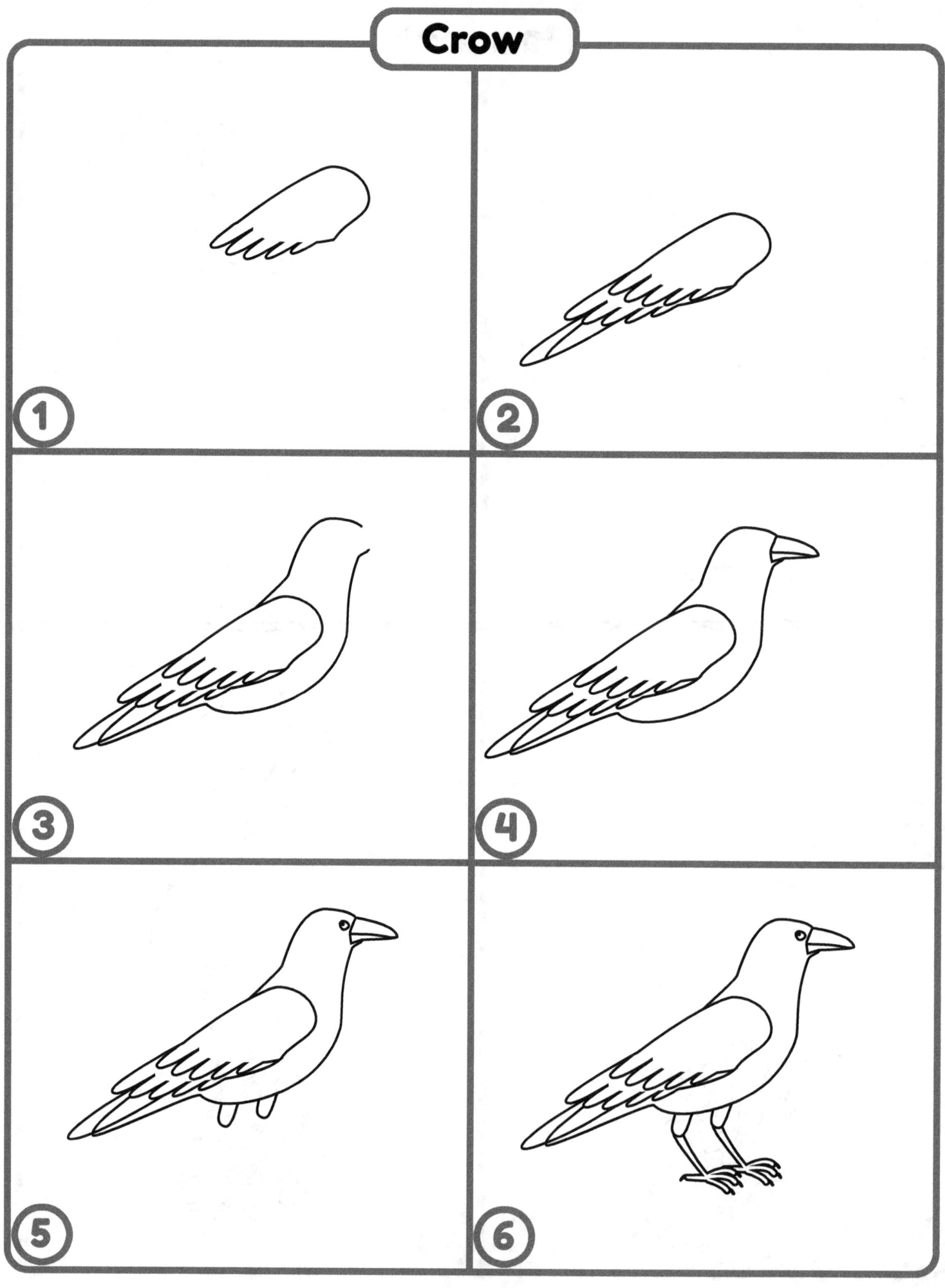

# Goose

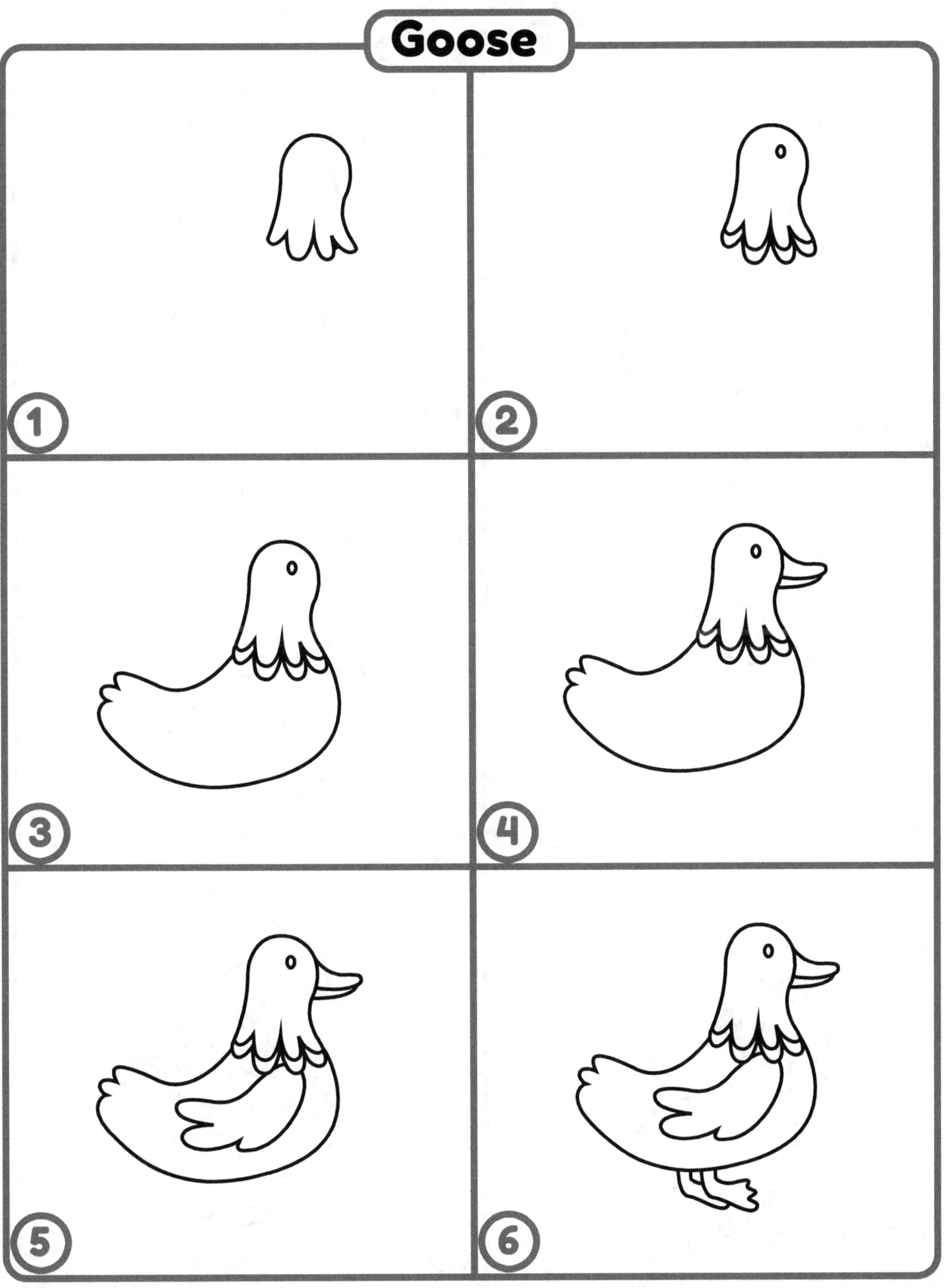

# Parrot

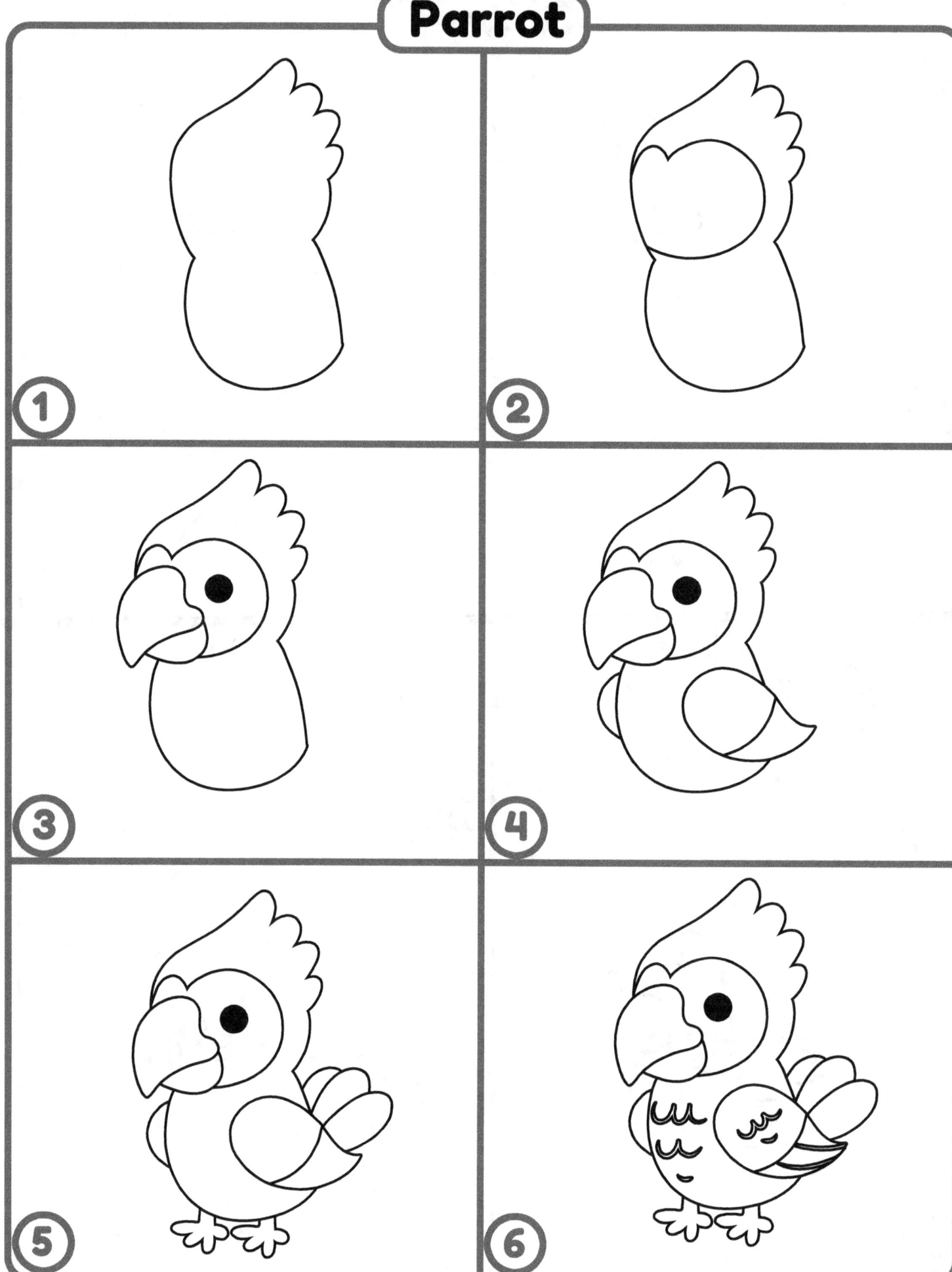

# Owl

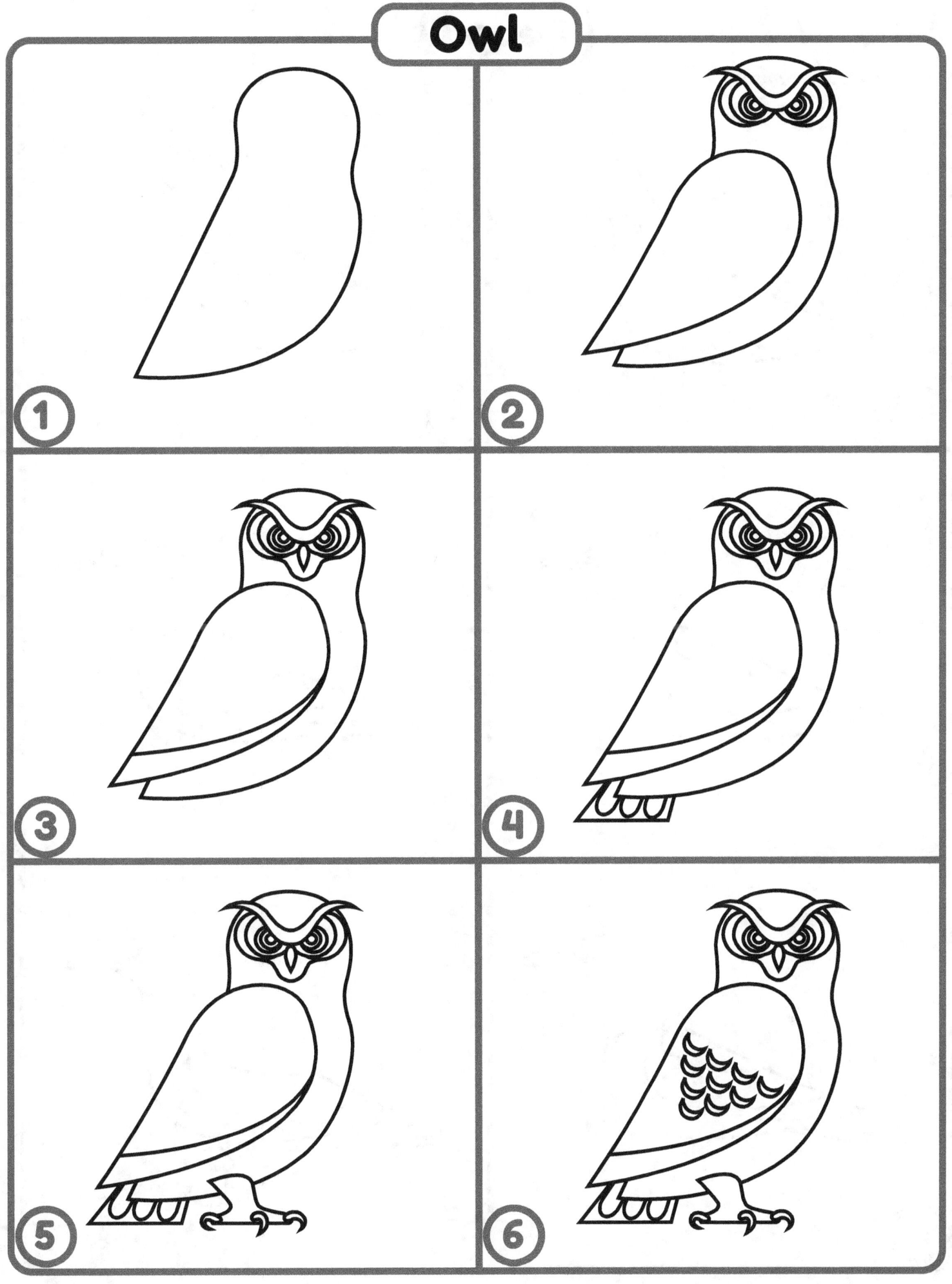

# Seagull

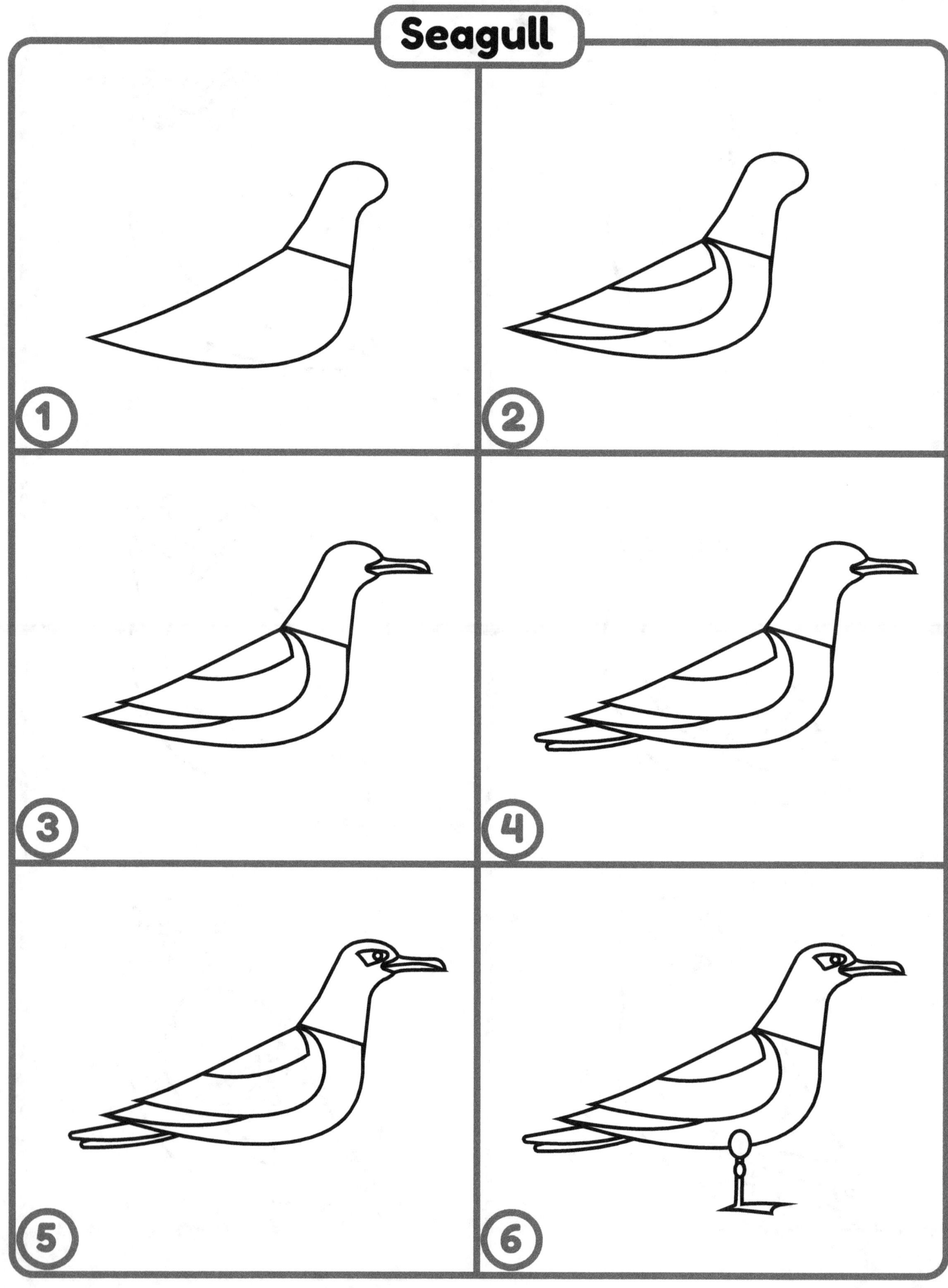

# Penguin

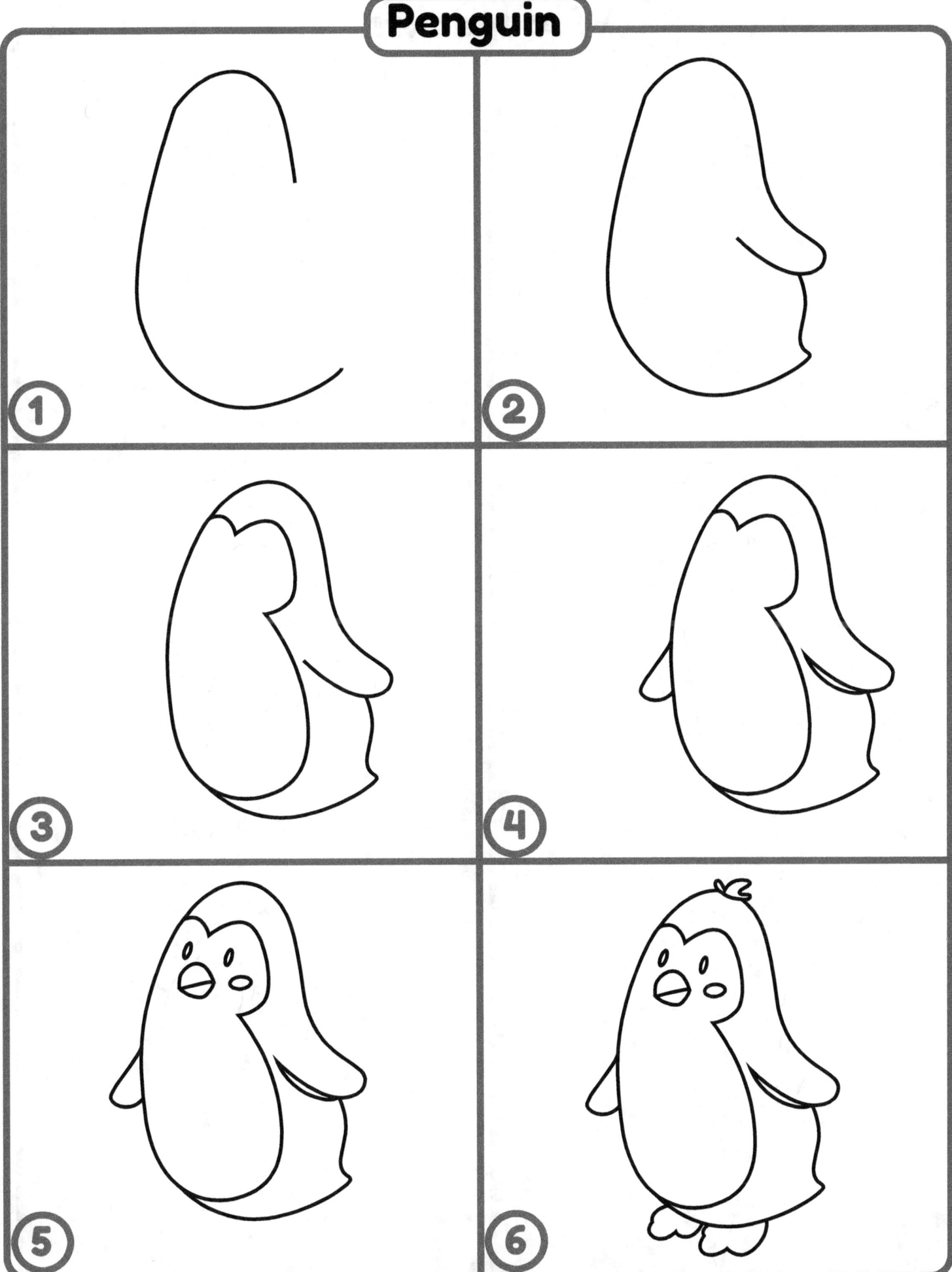

# Woodpecker

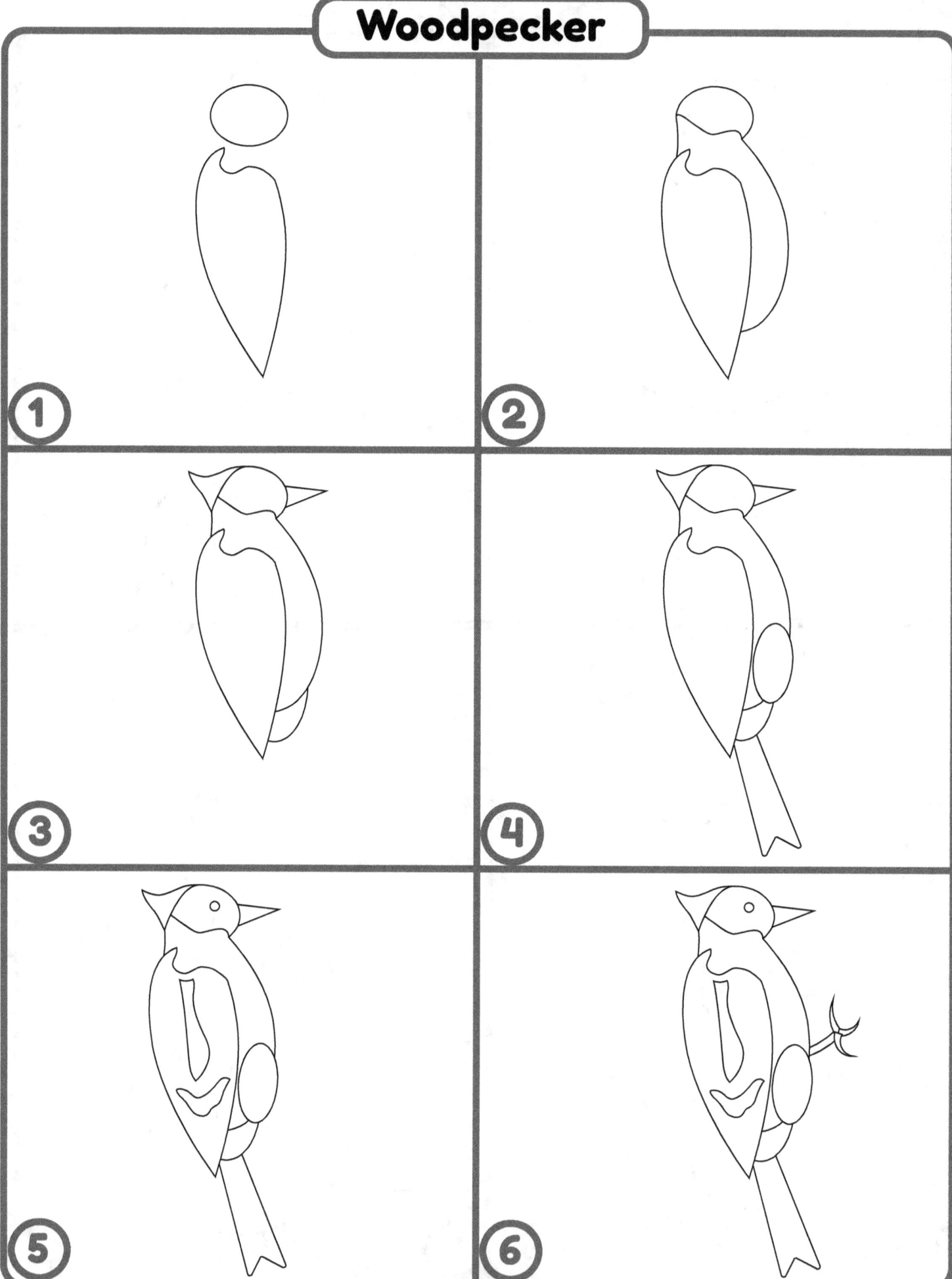

# Flamingo

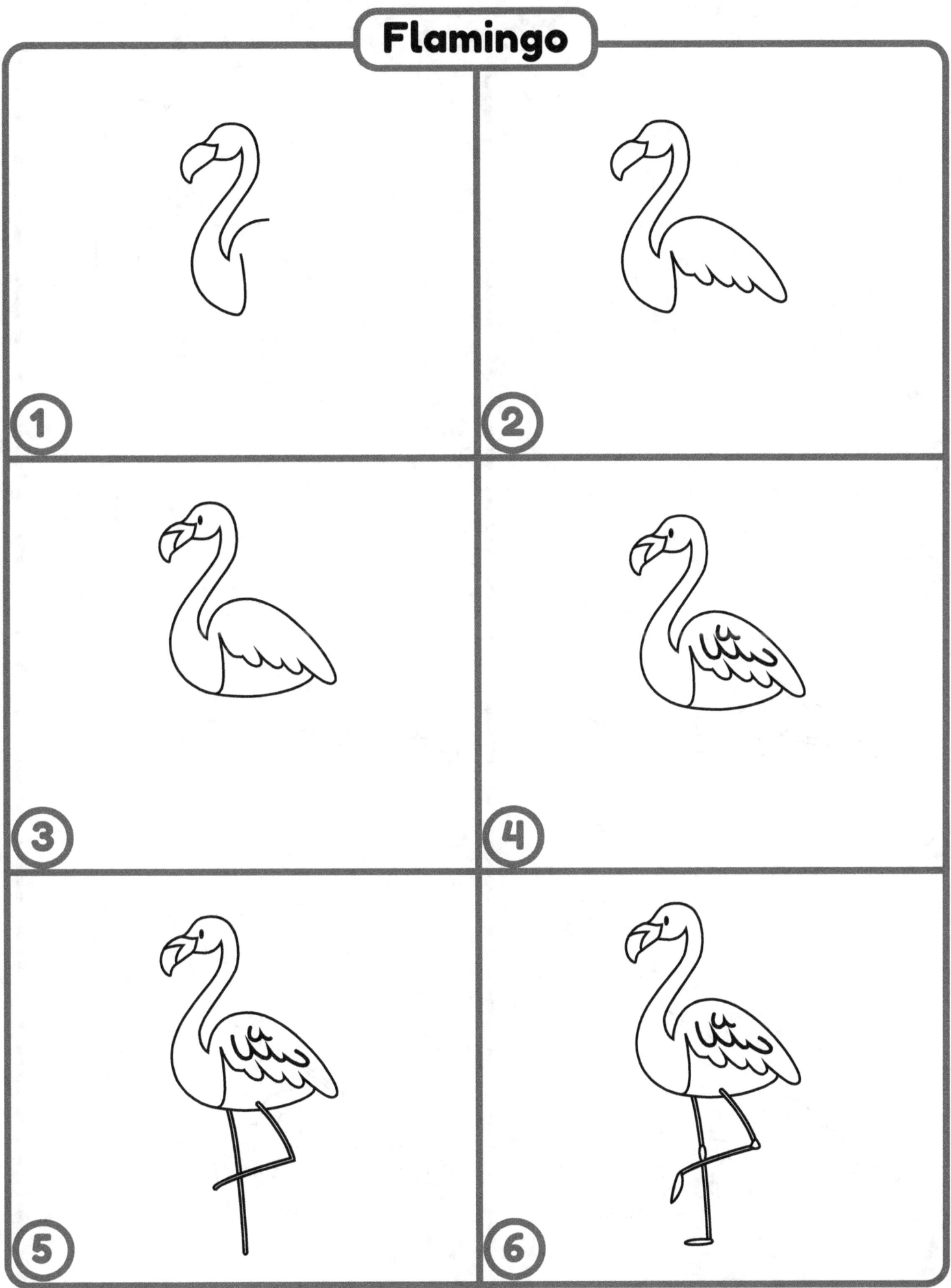

# Pigeon

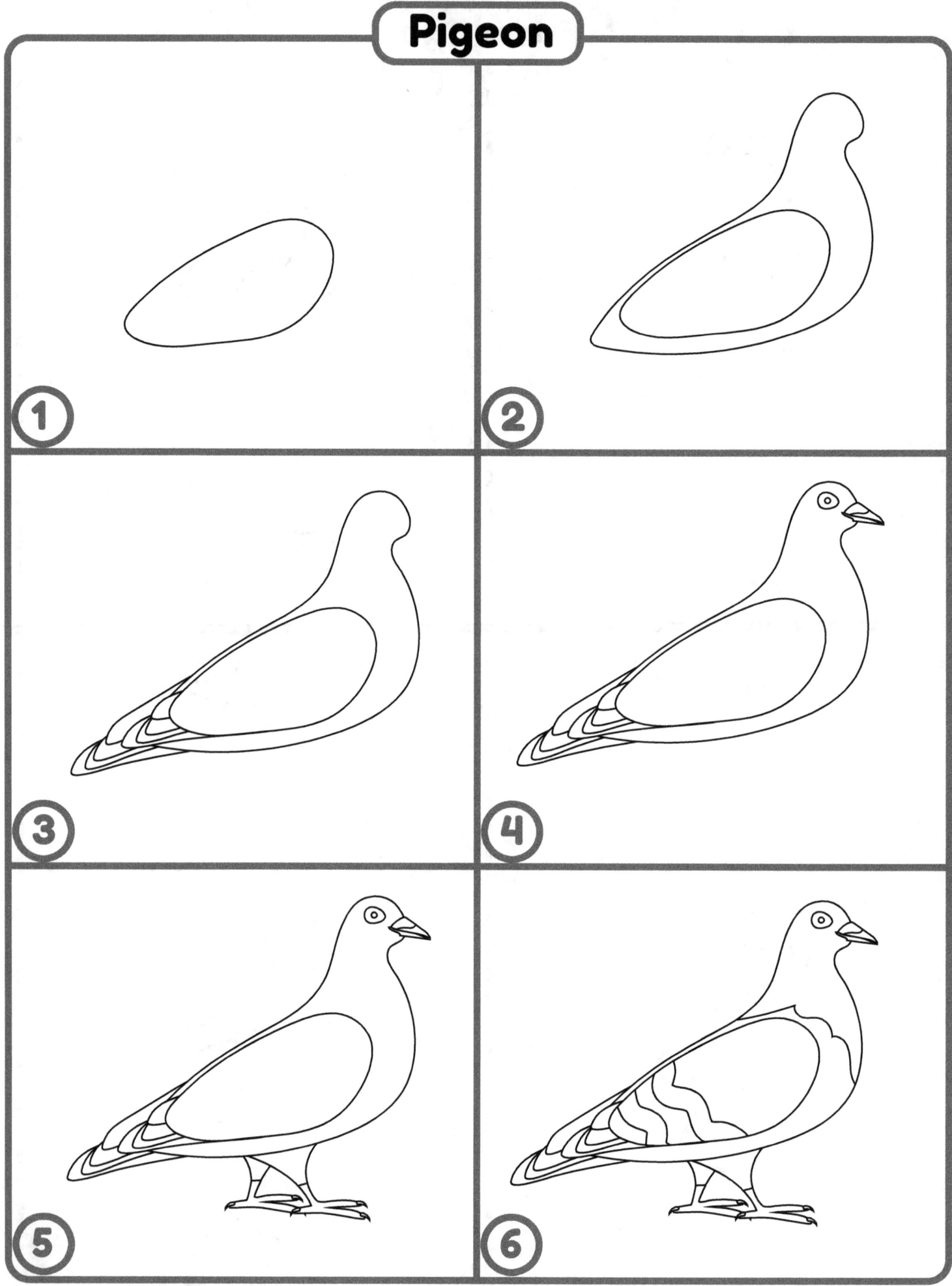

# Wild Animals

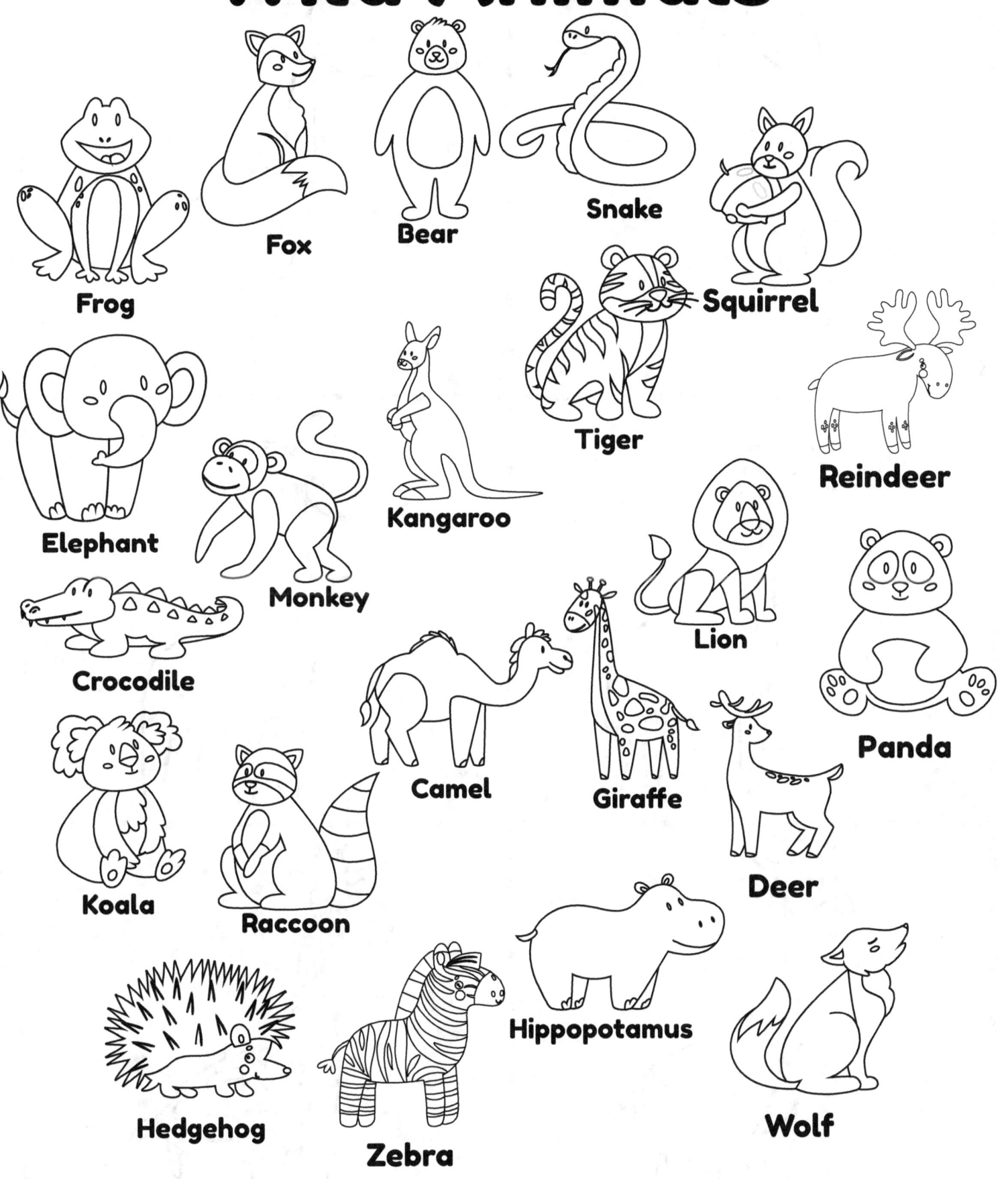

Frog

Fox

Bear

Snake

Squirrel

Tiger

Reindeer

Elephant

Monkey

Kangaroo

Lion

Panda

Crocodile

Camel

Giraffe

Deer

Koala

Raccoon

Hippopotamus

Hedgehog

Zebra

Wolf

# Giraffe

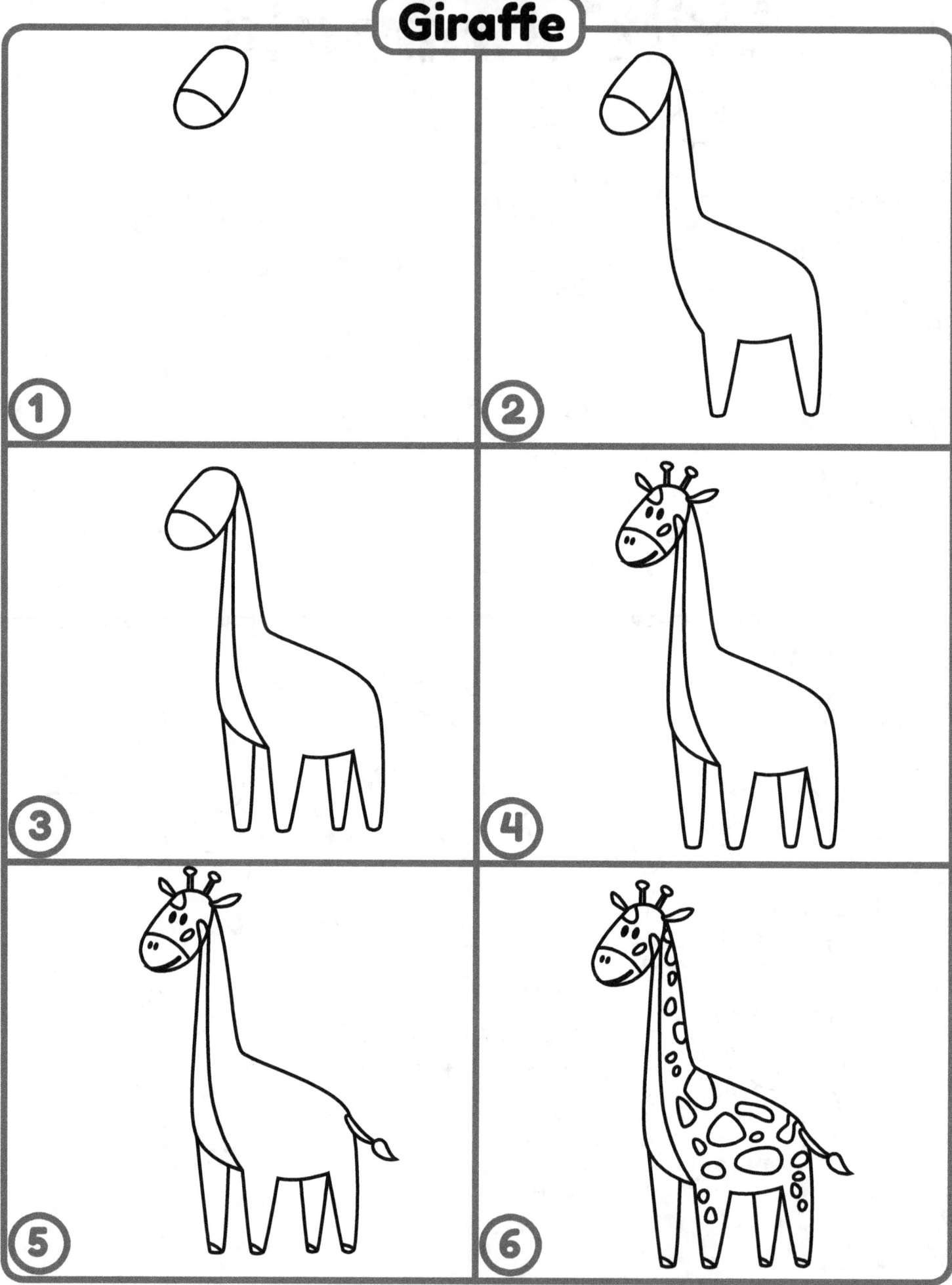

# Tiger

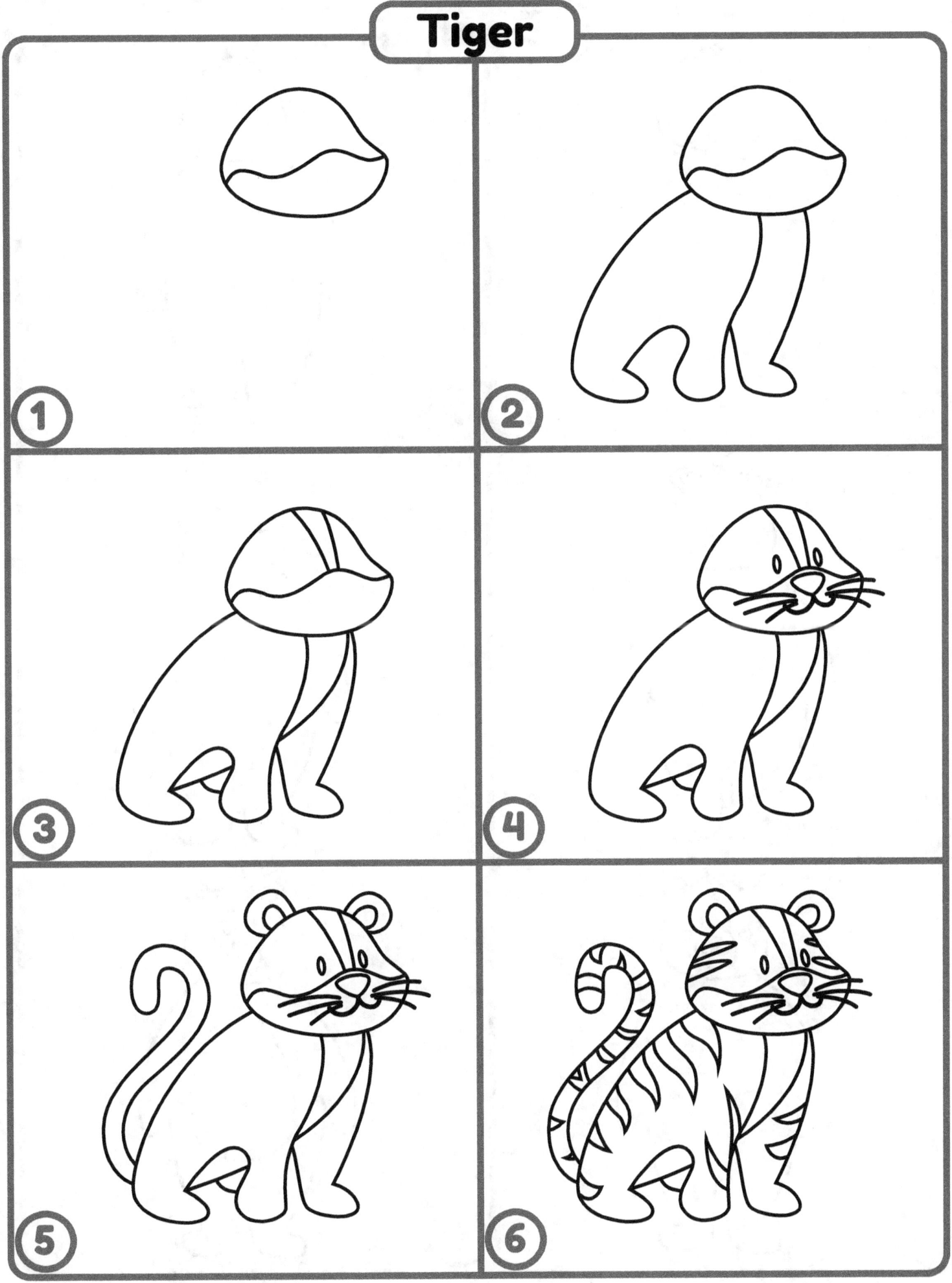

# Bear

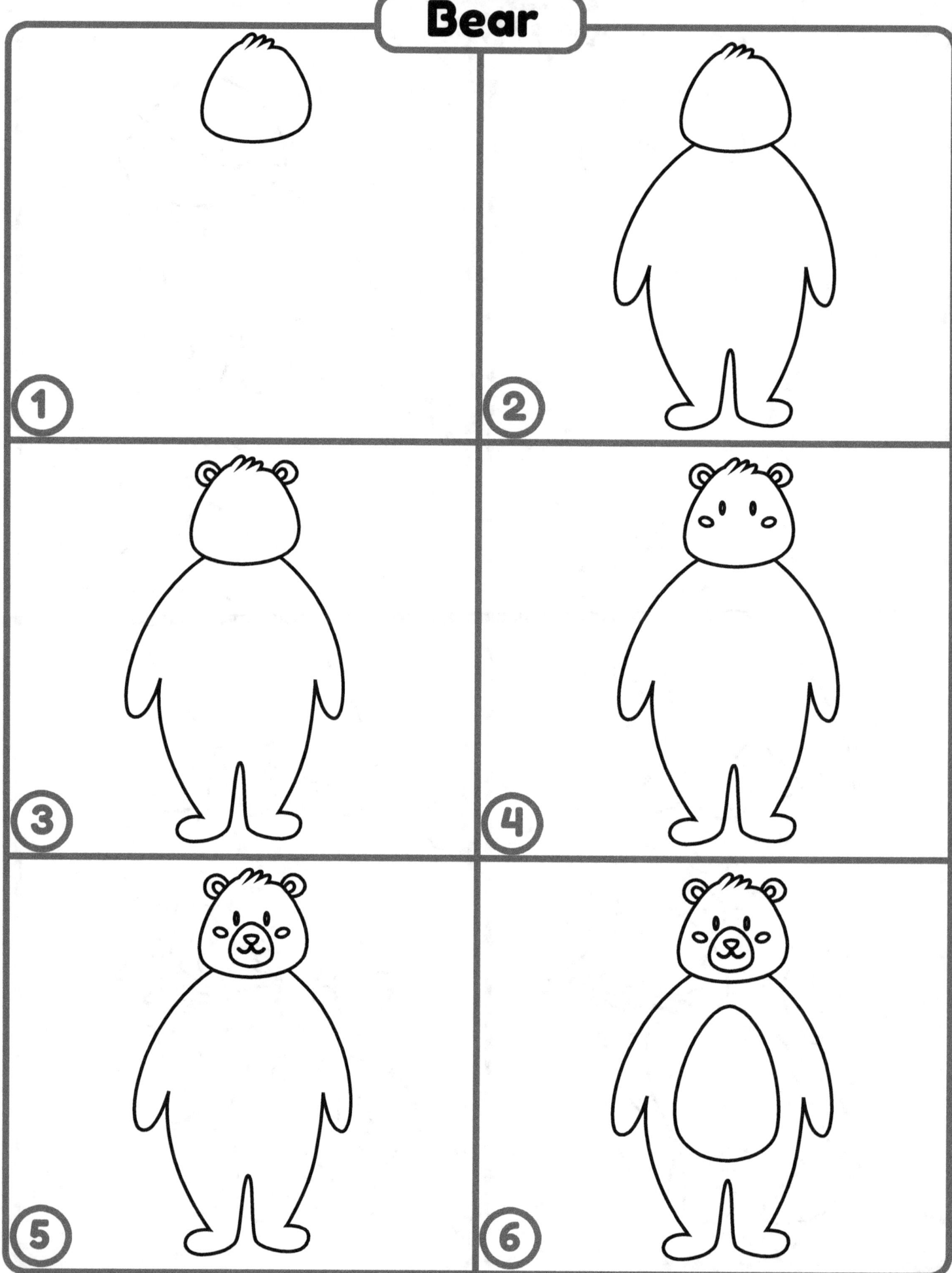

# Lion

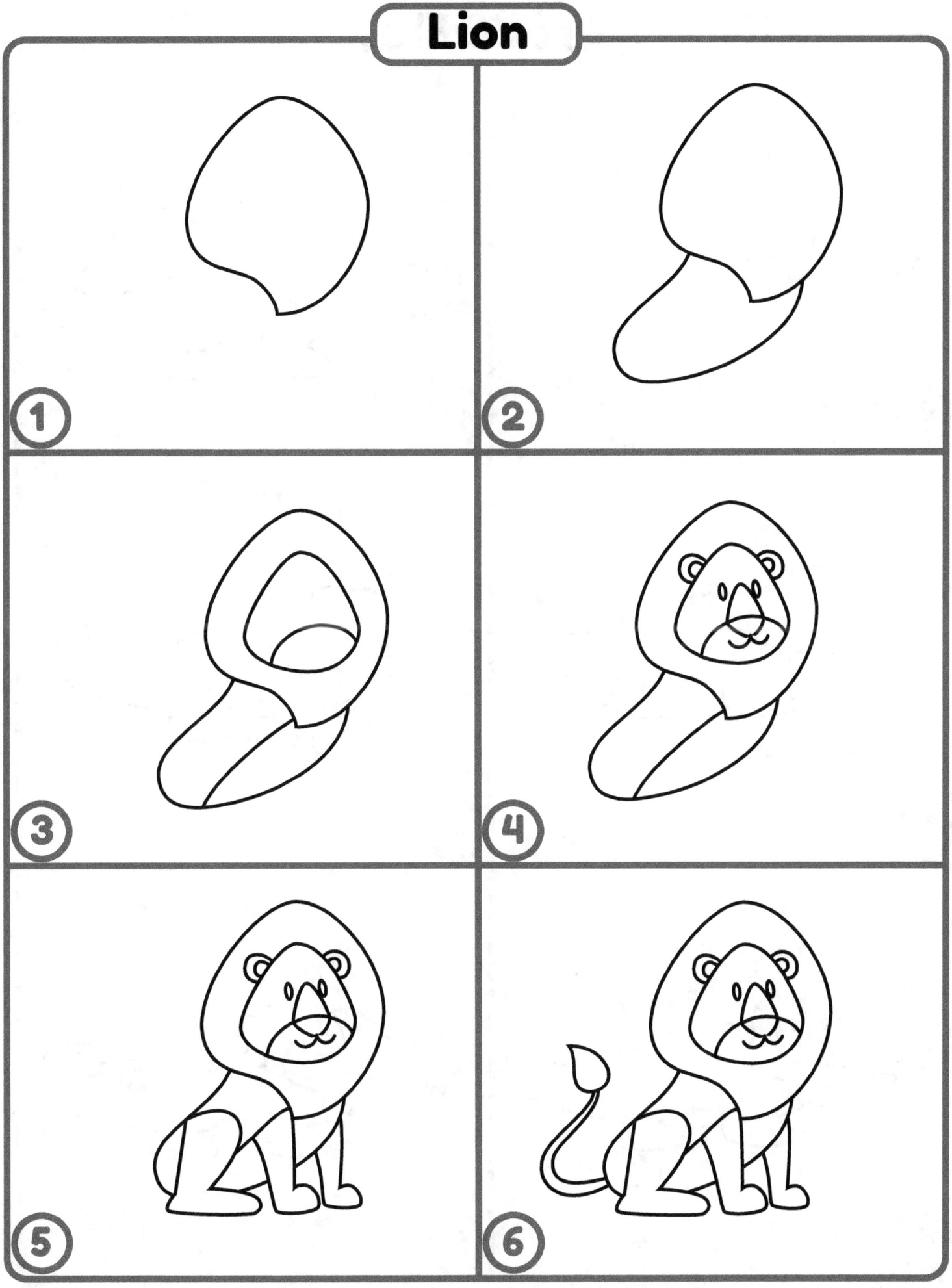

# Crocodile

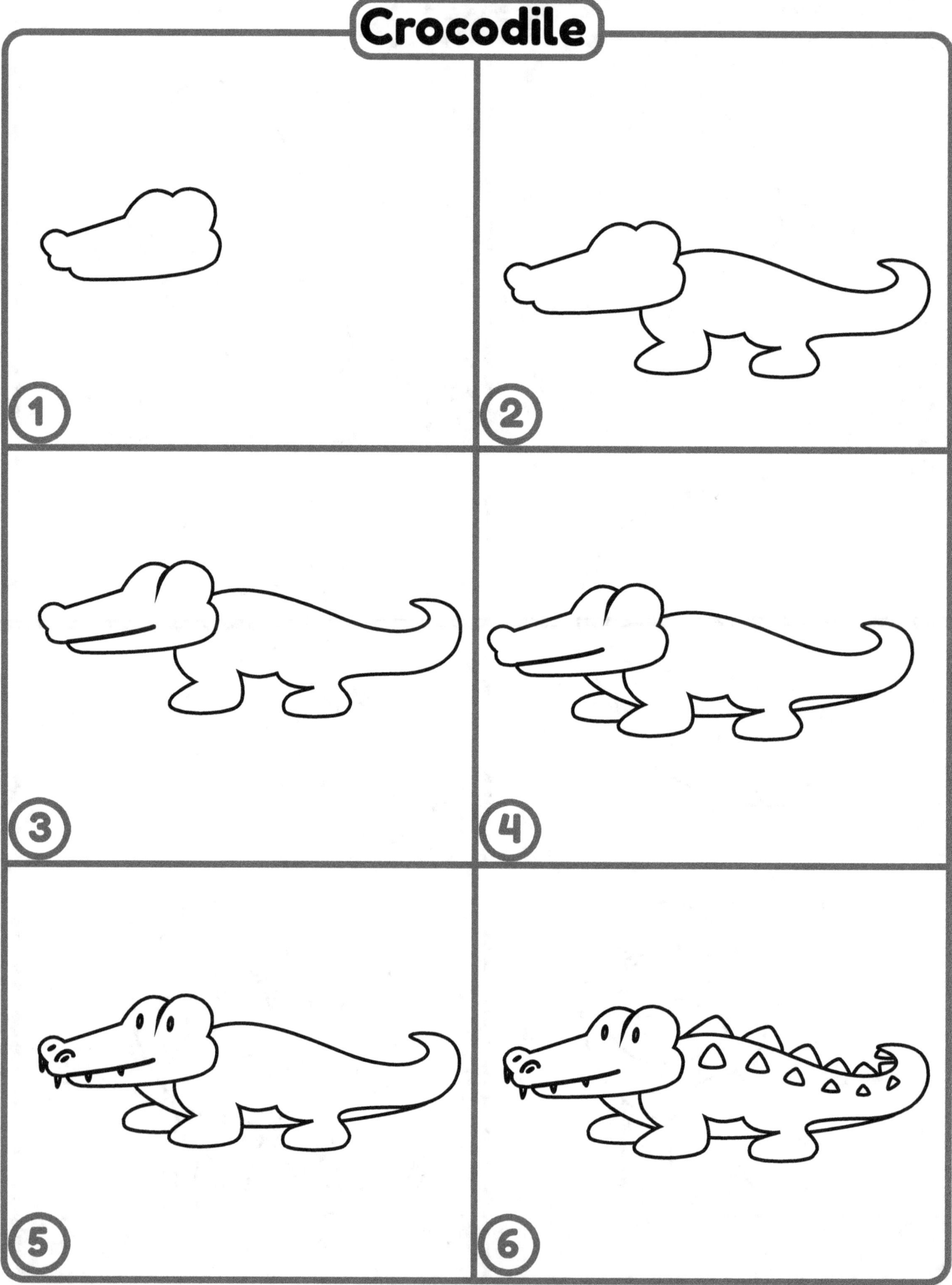

# Elephant

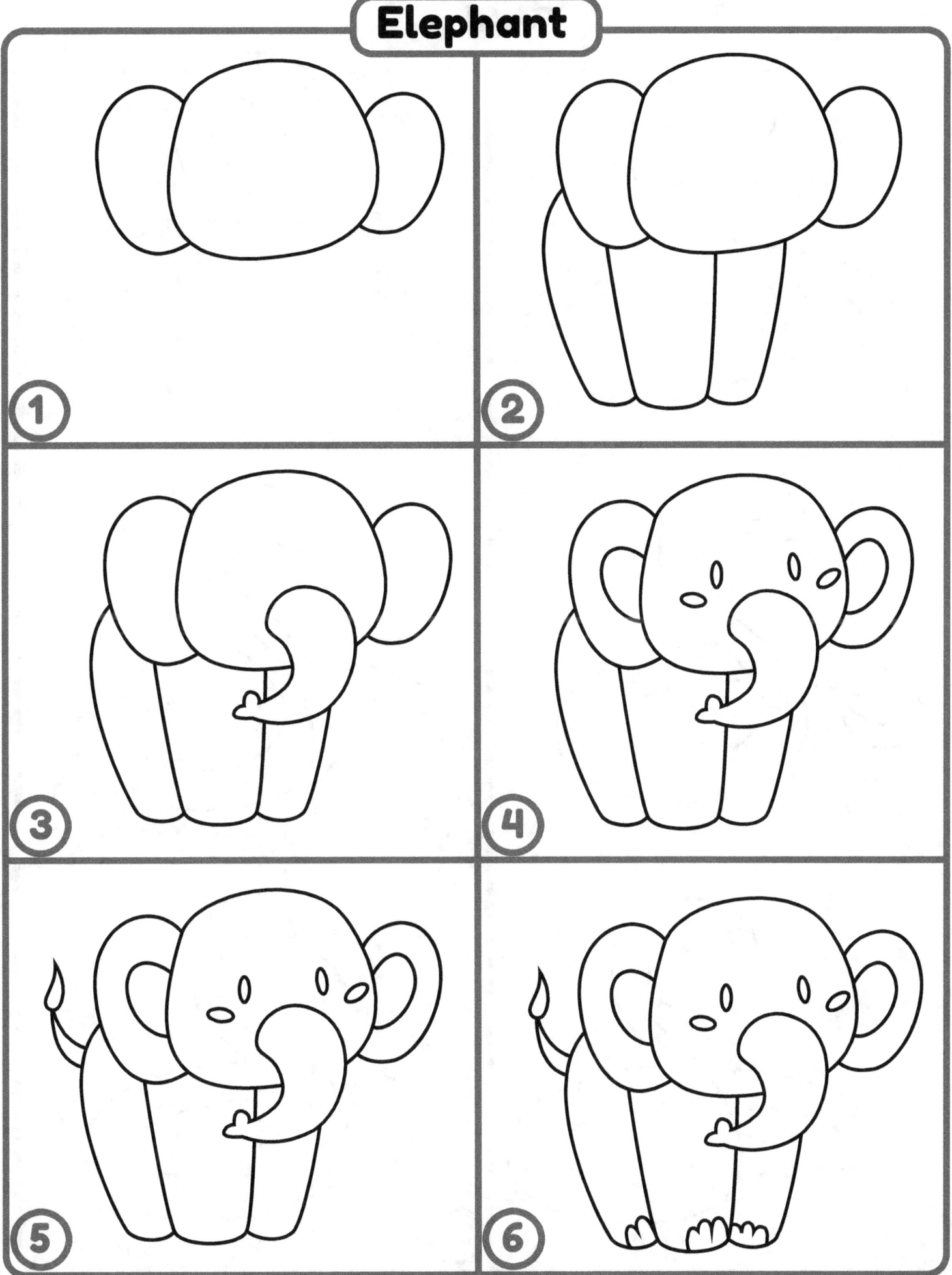

# Snake

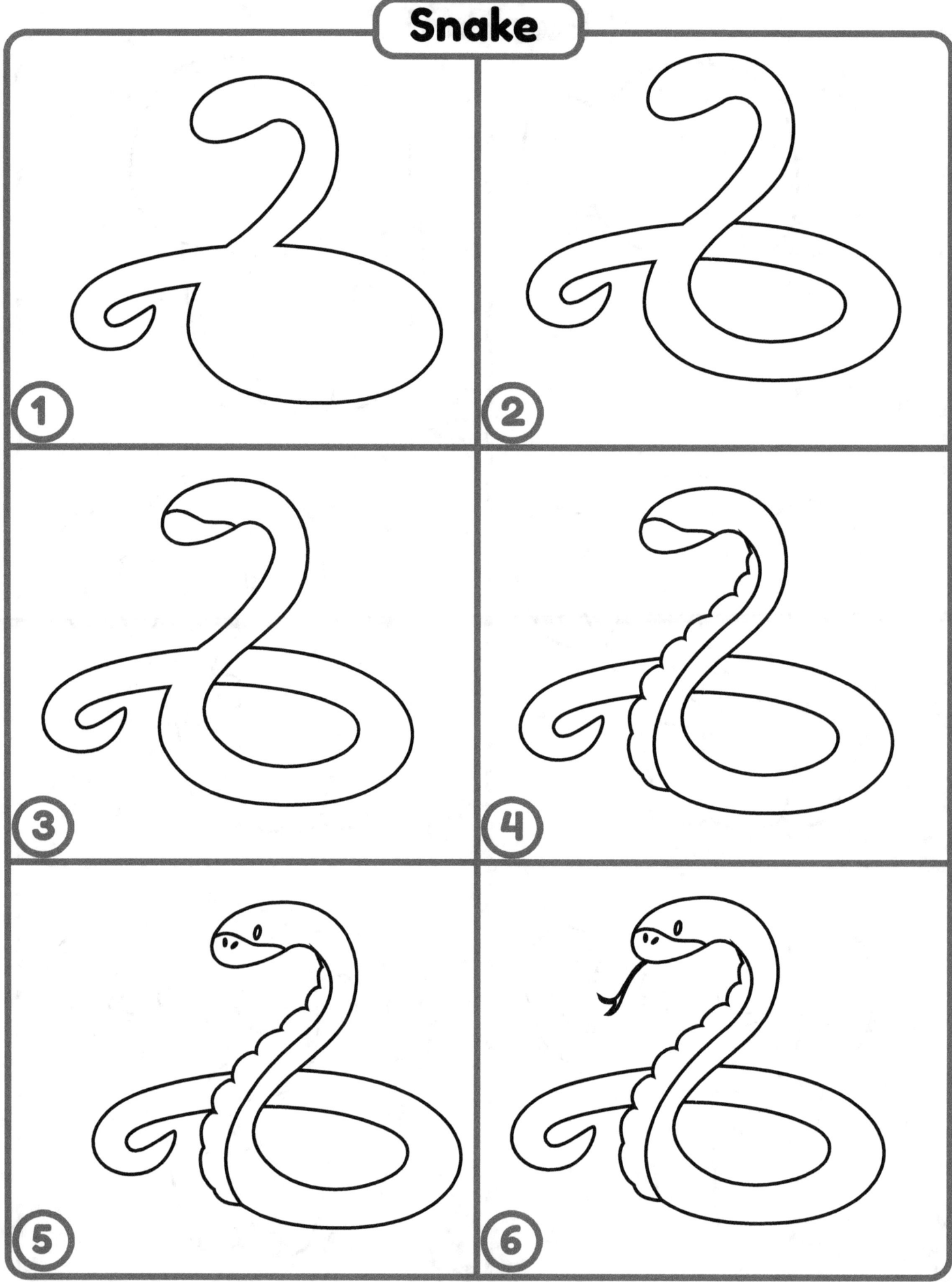

# Fox

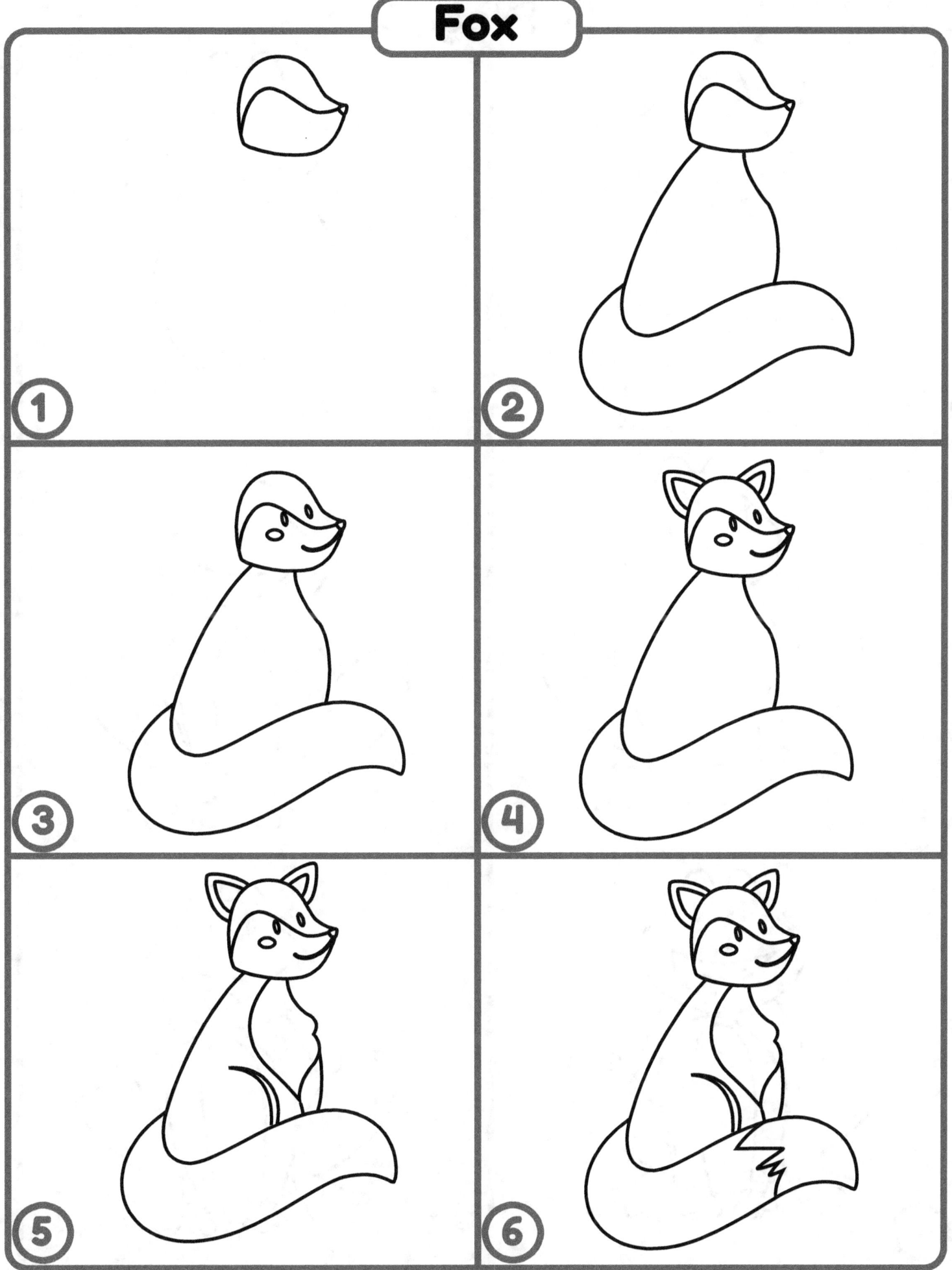

# Frog

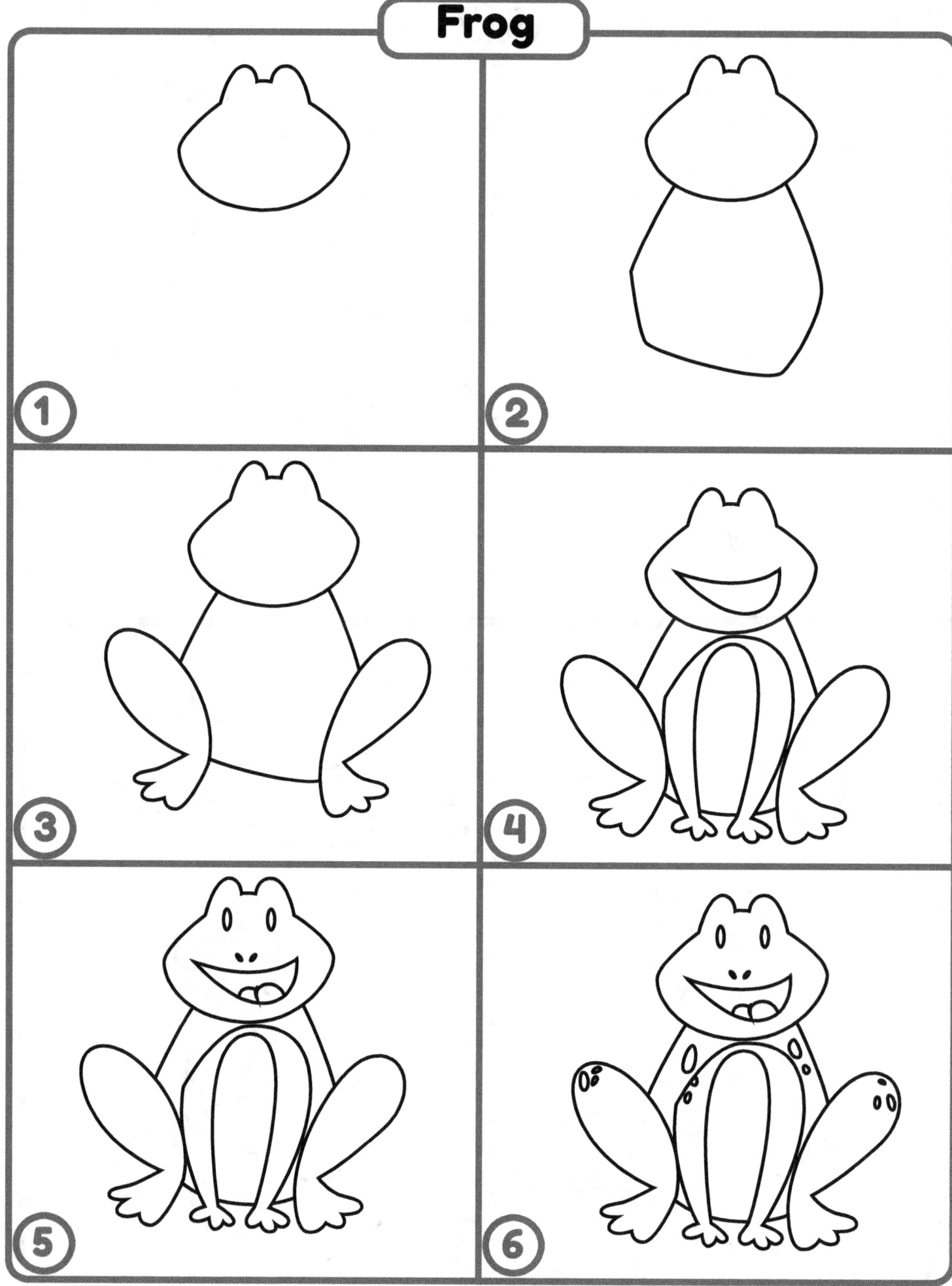

# Zebra

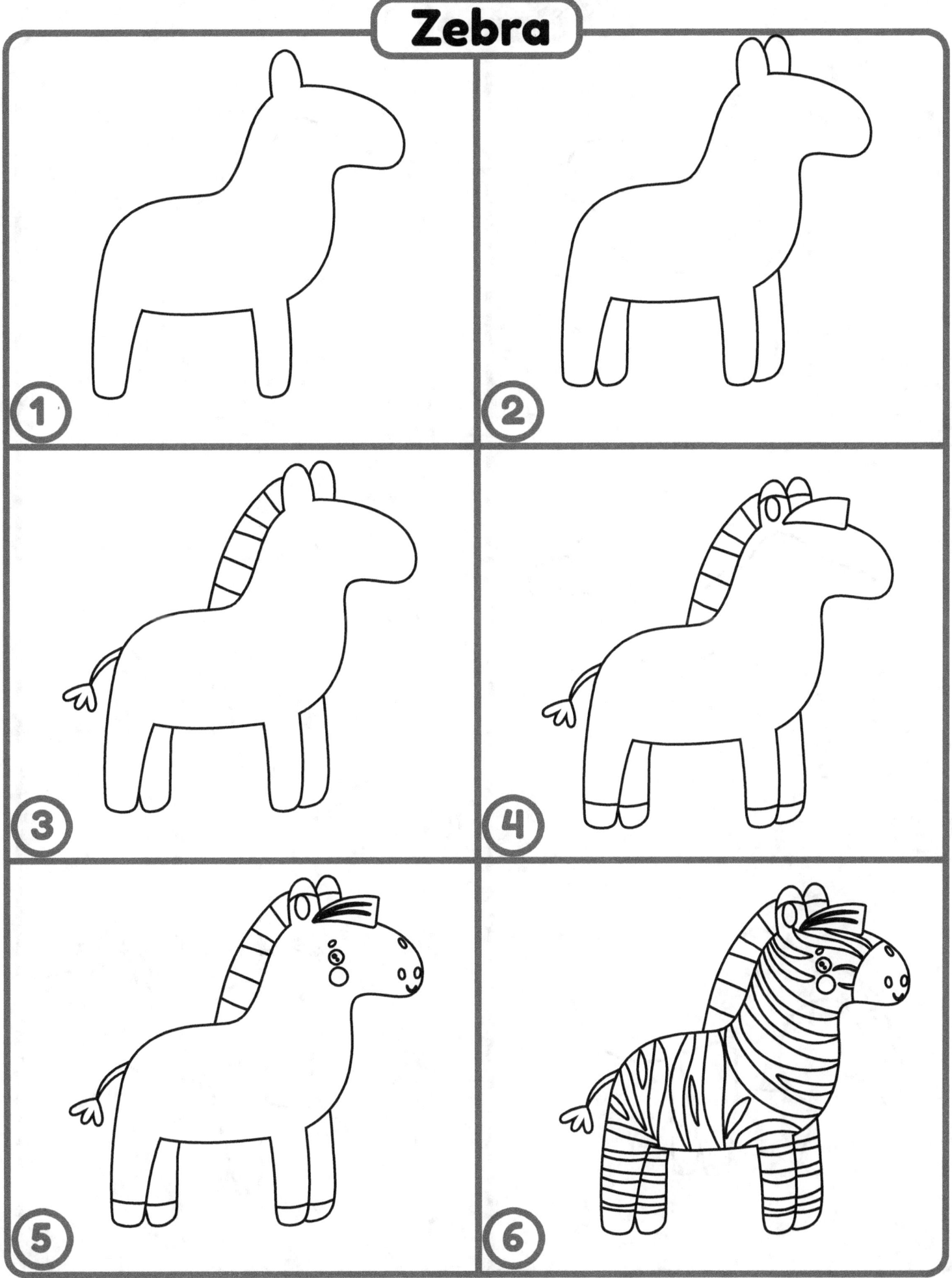

# Camel

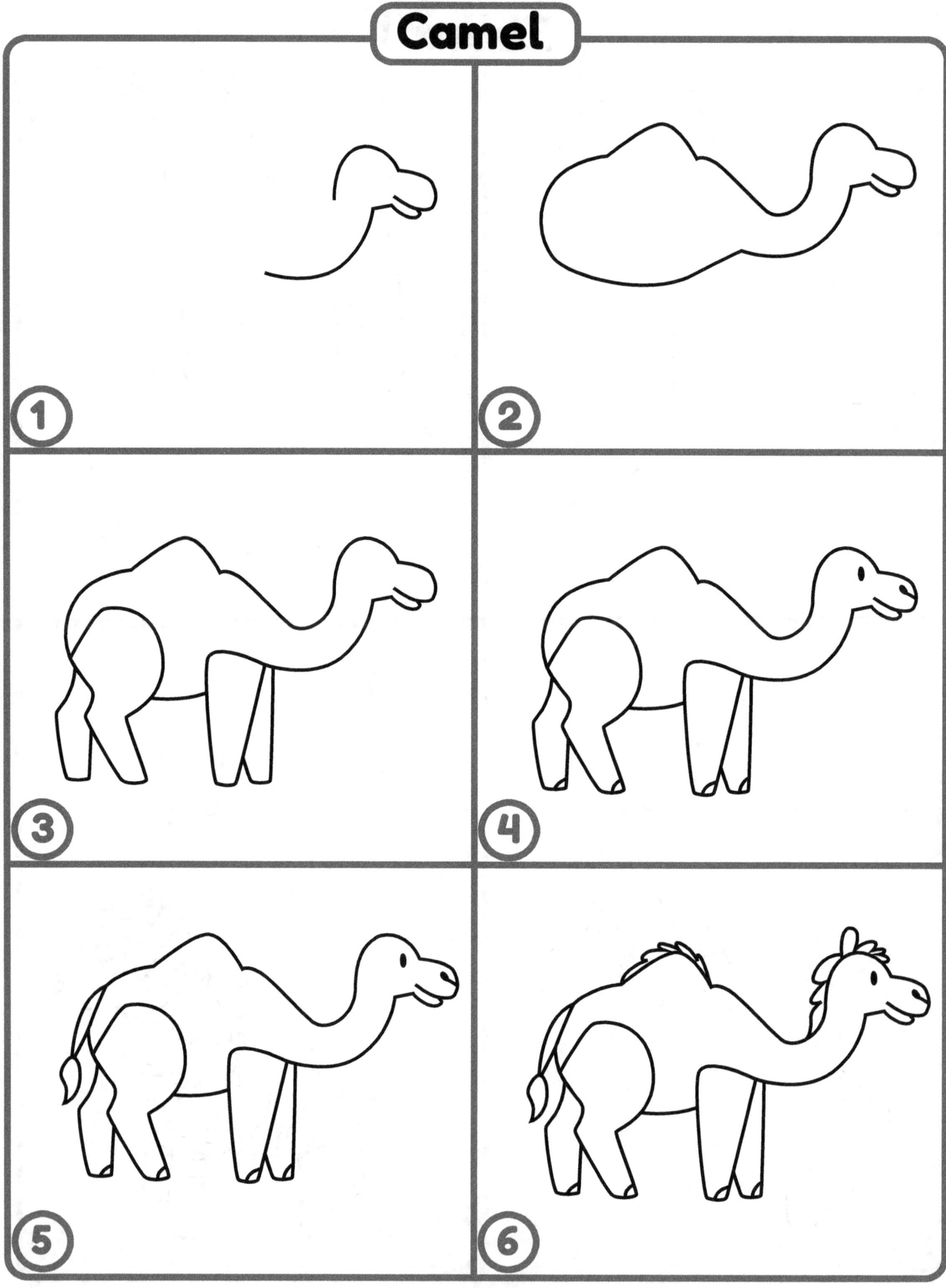

# Squirrel

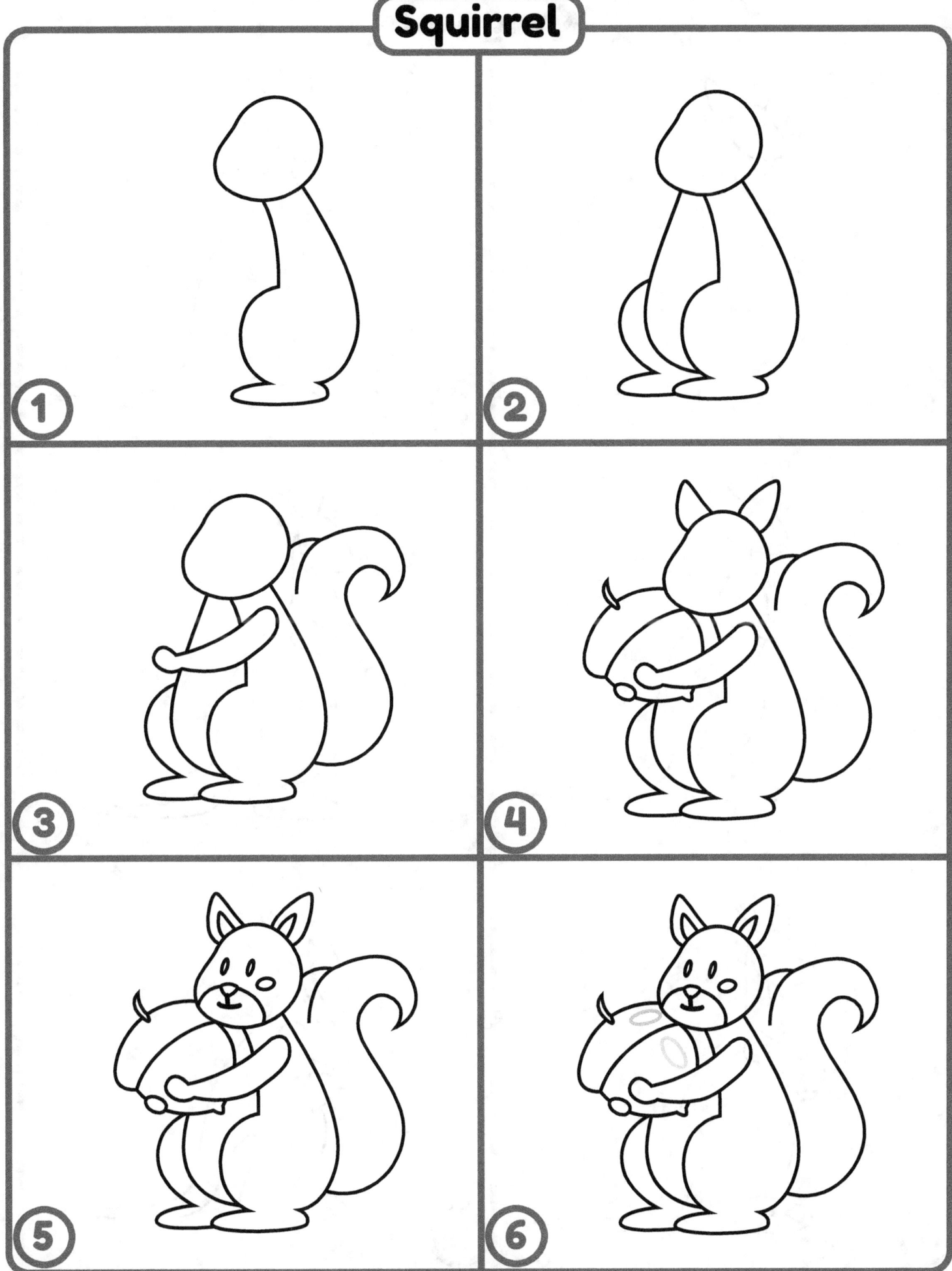

# Kangaroo

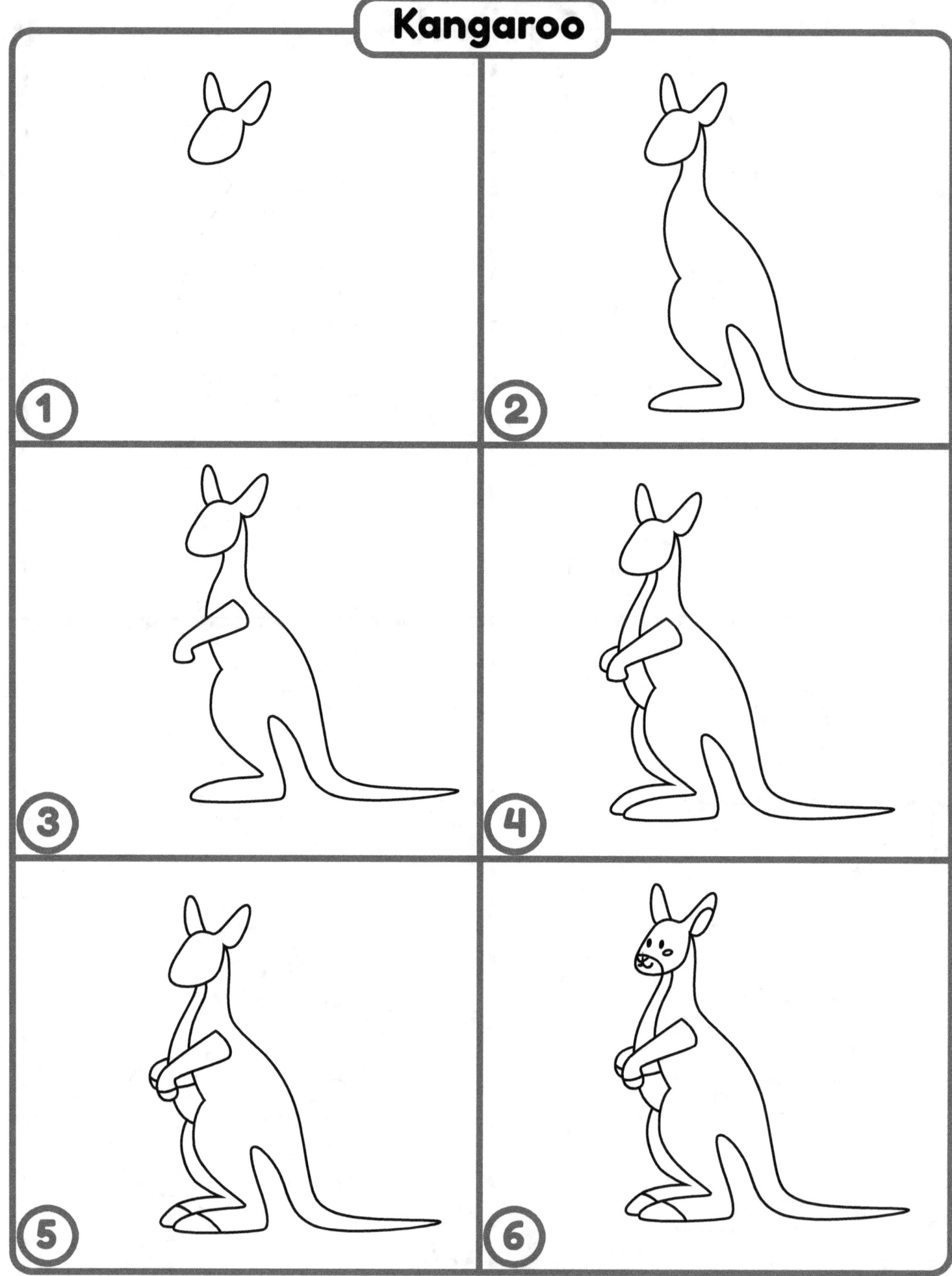

# Hippopotamus

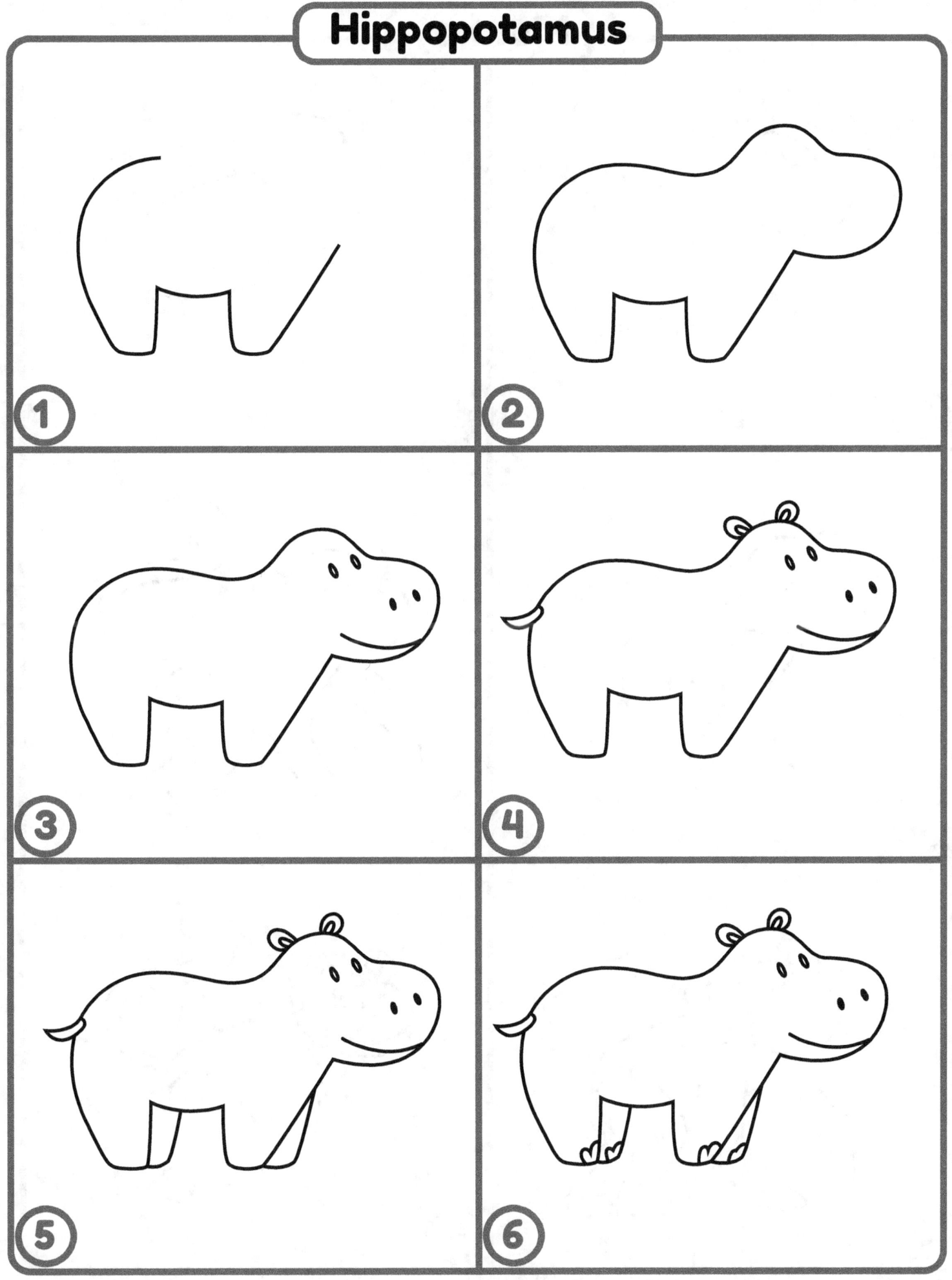

# Monkey

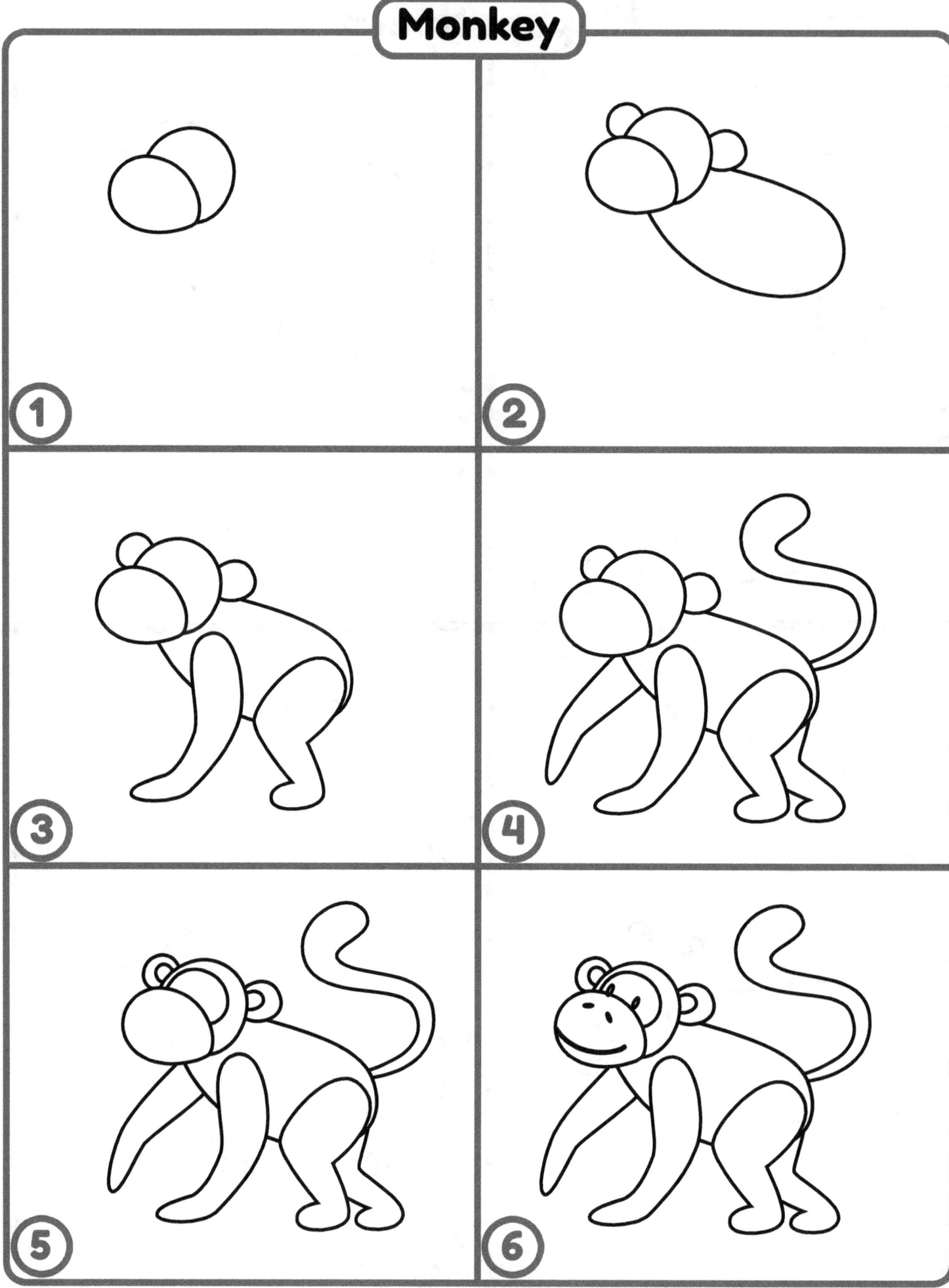

# Hedgehog

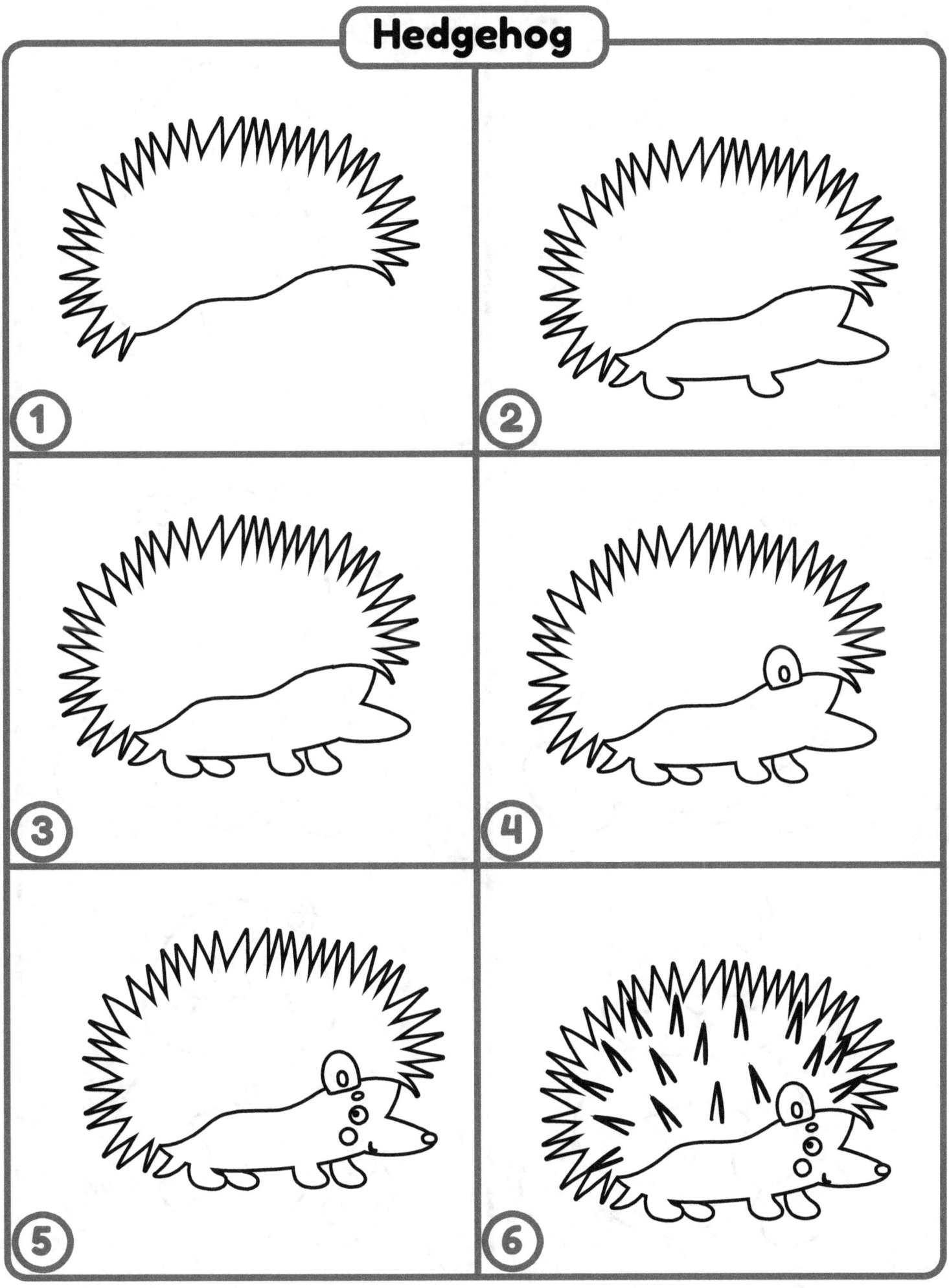

# Panda

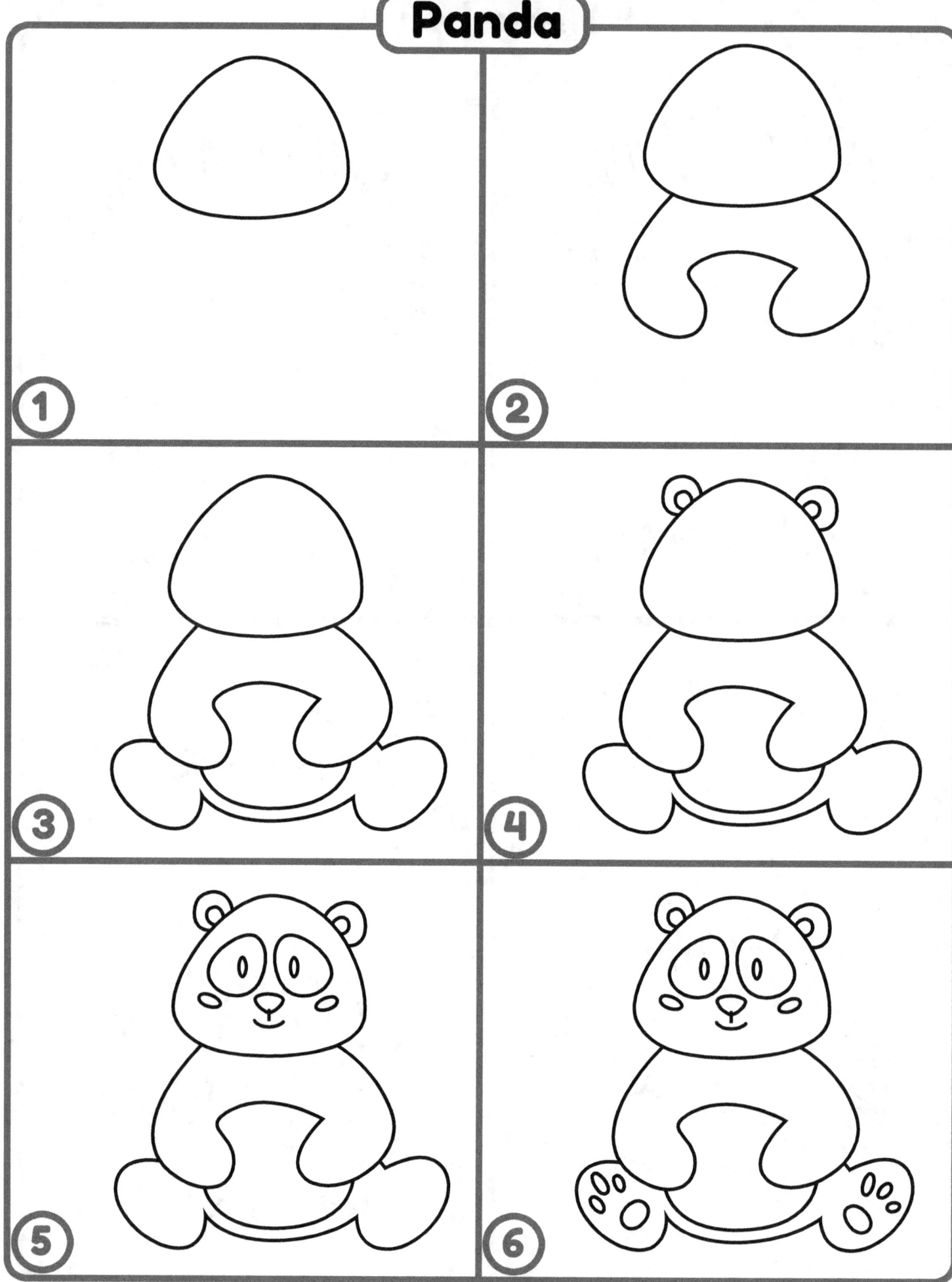

# Reindeer

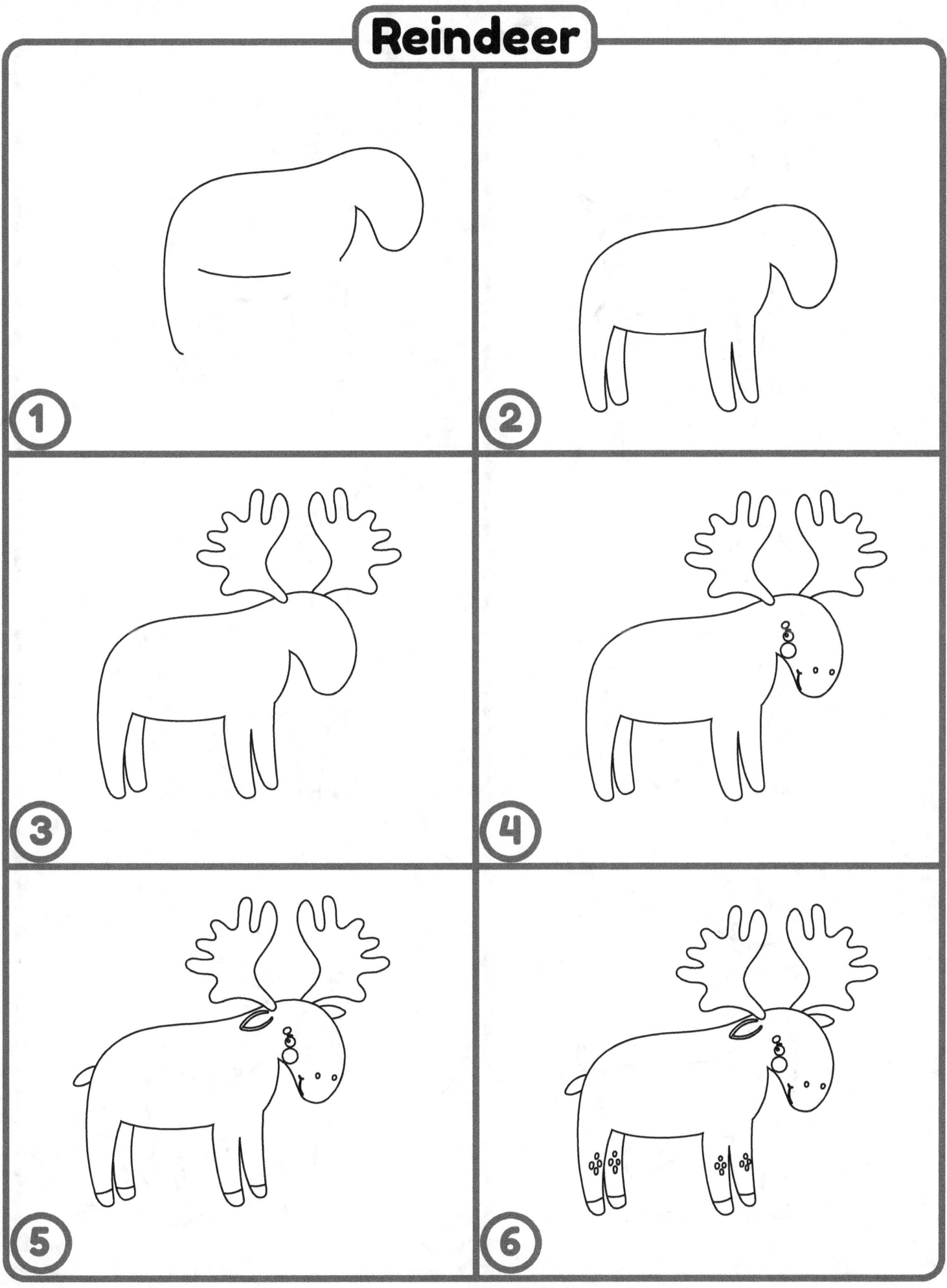

# Deer

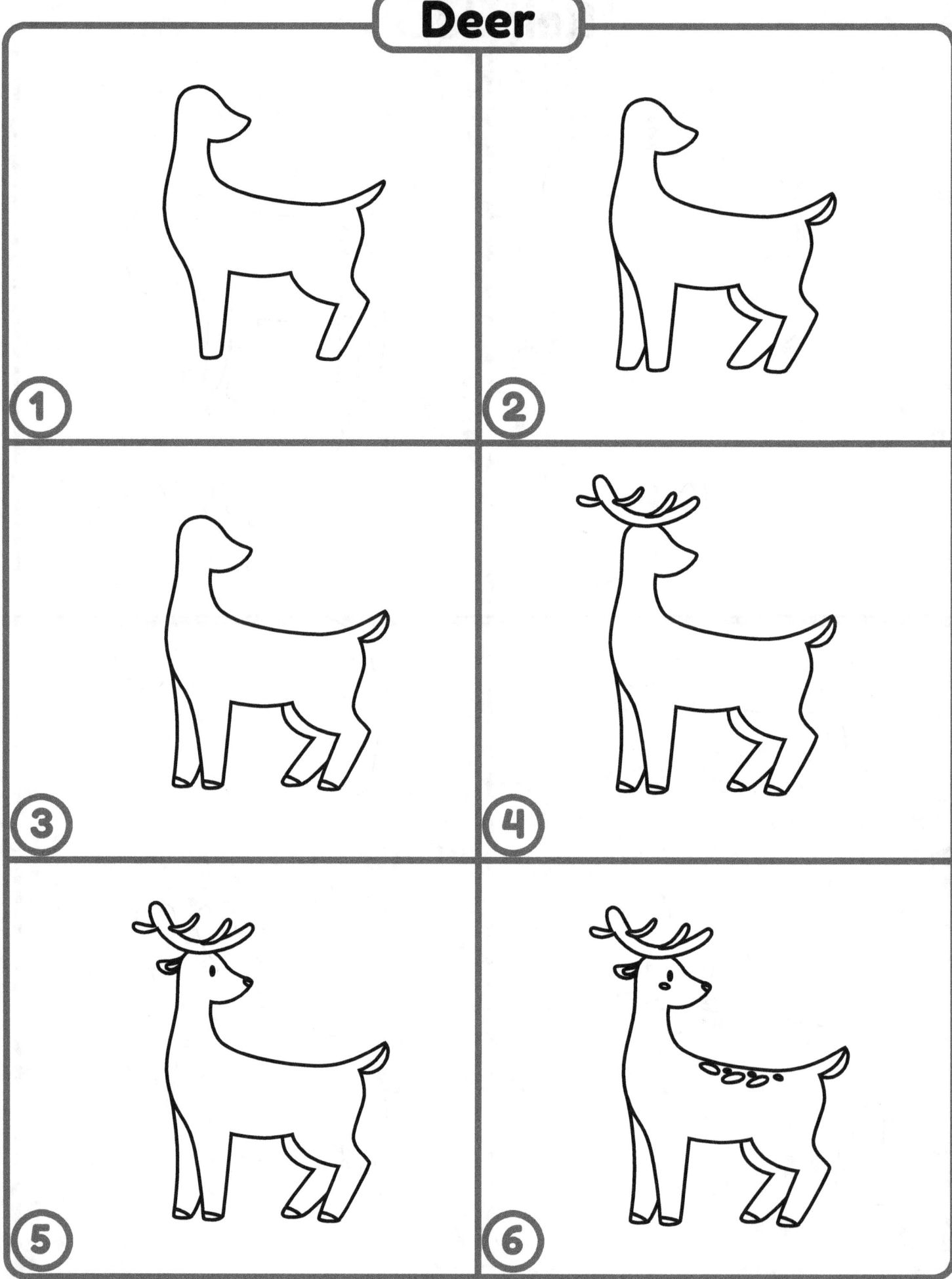

# Wolf

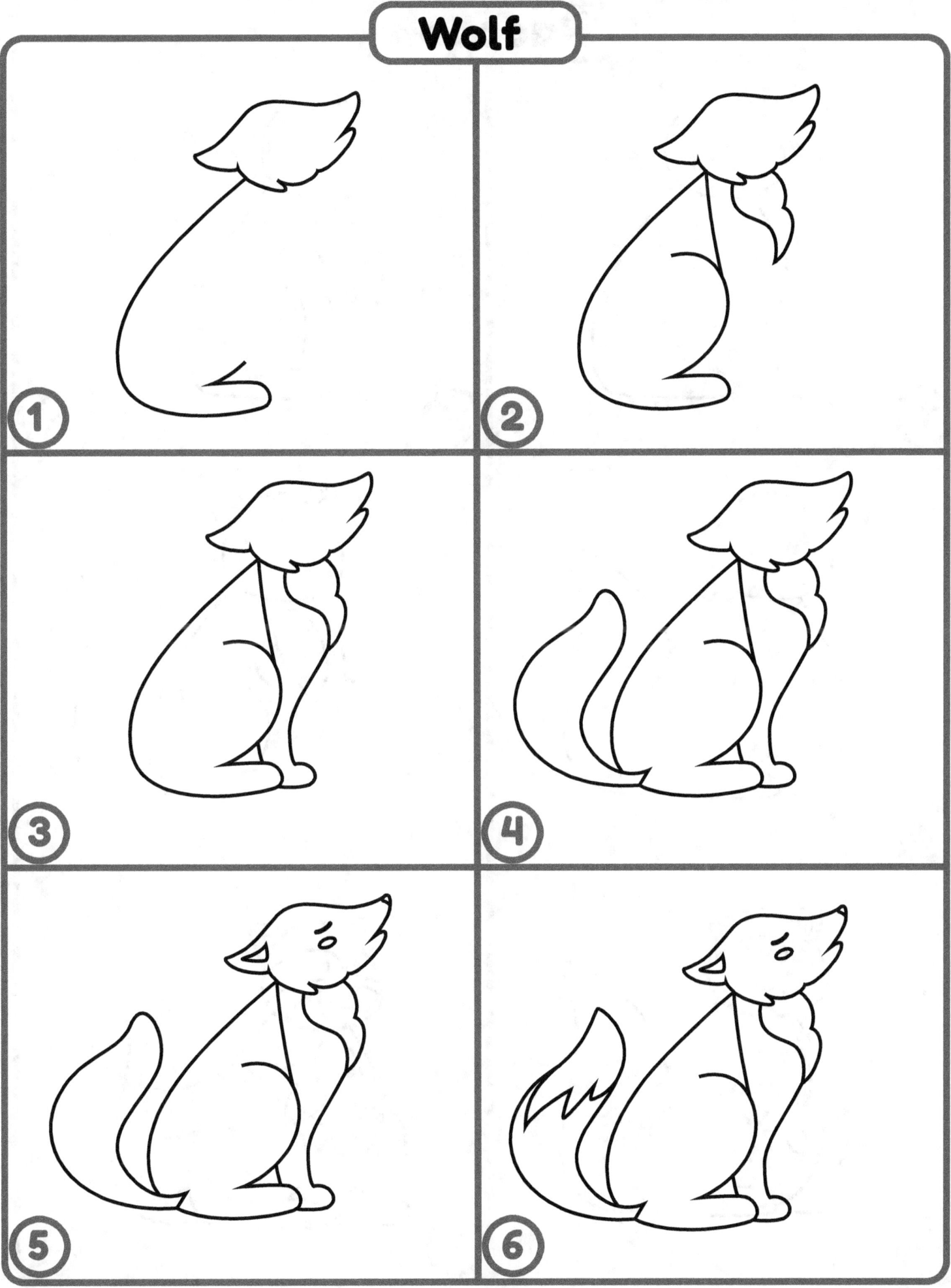

# Raccoon

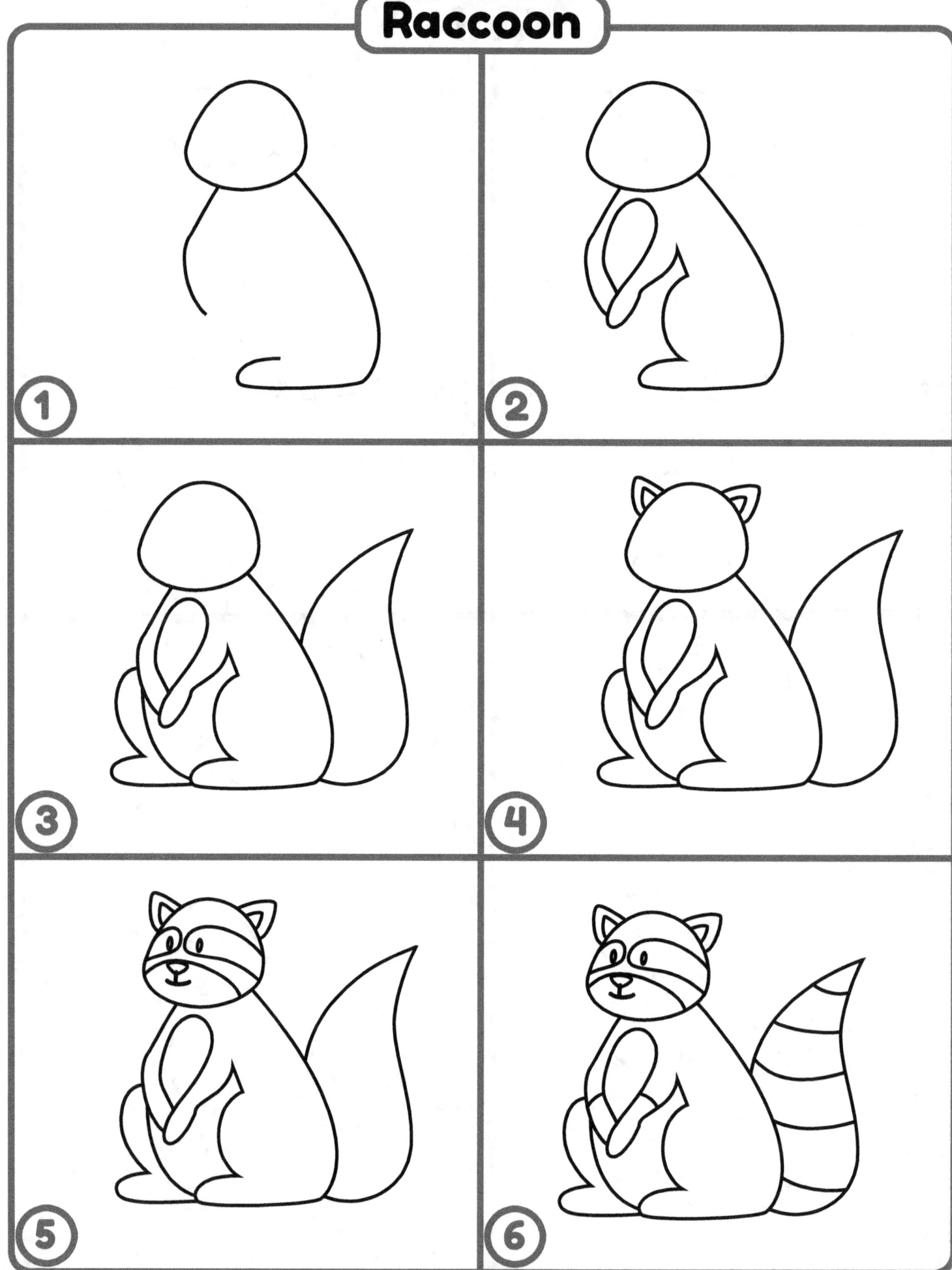

# Koala

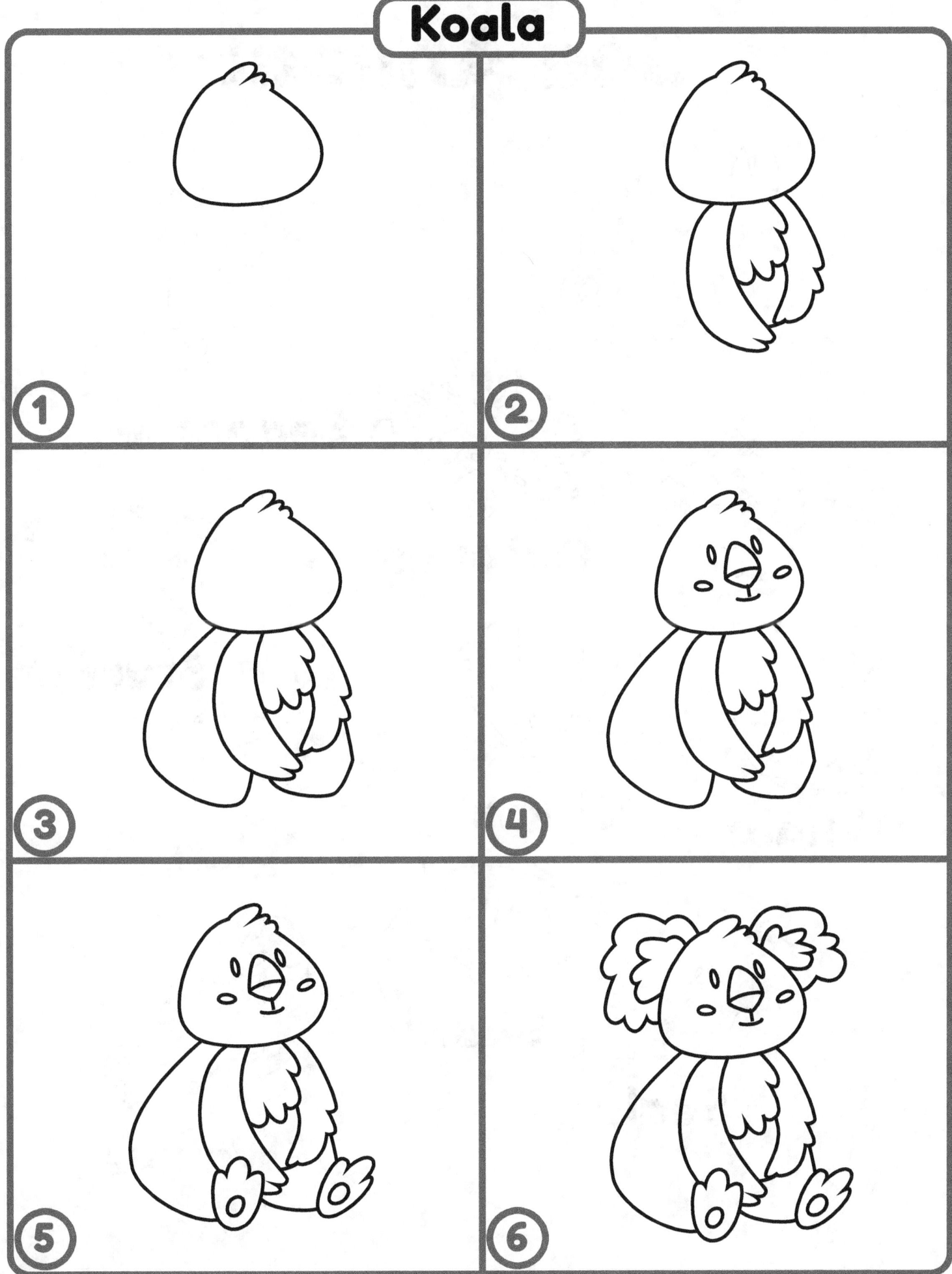

# Sea Animal

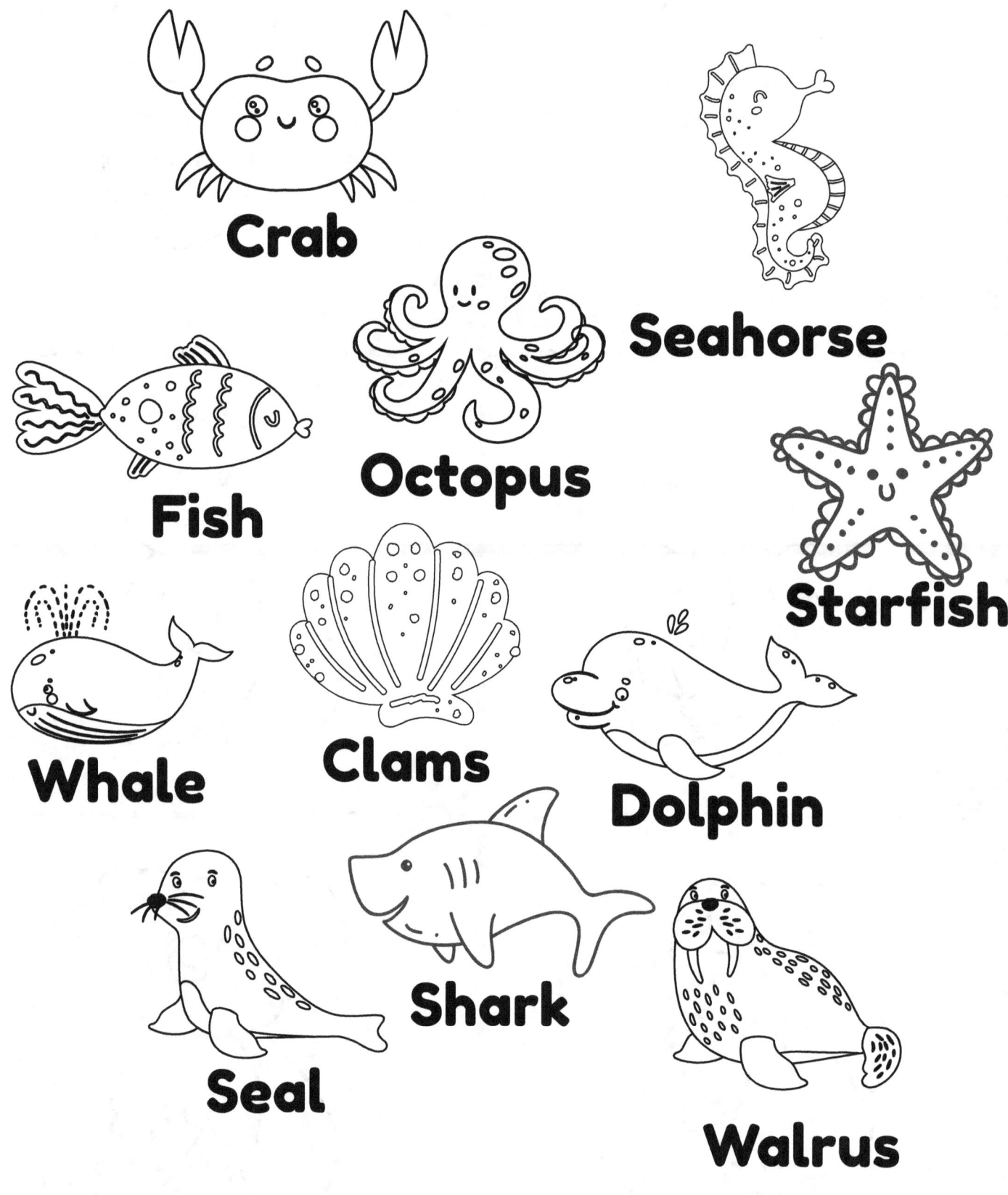

Crab

Seahorse

Octopus

Fish

Starfish

Whale

Clams

Dolphin

Seal

Shark

Walrus

# Crab

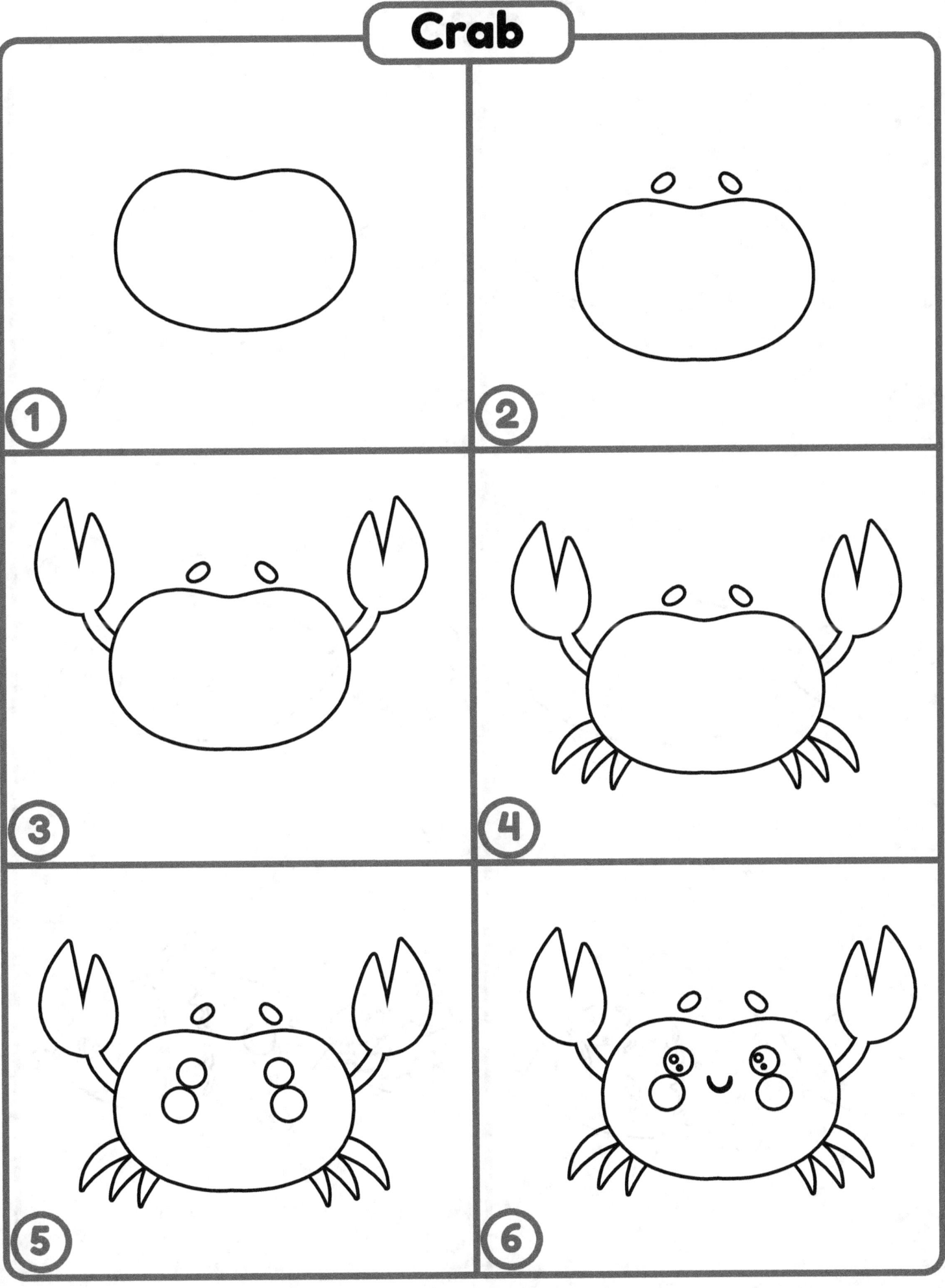

# Fish

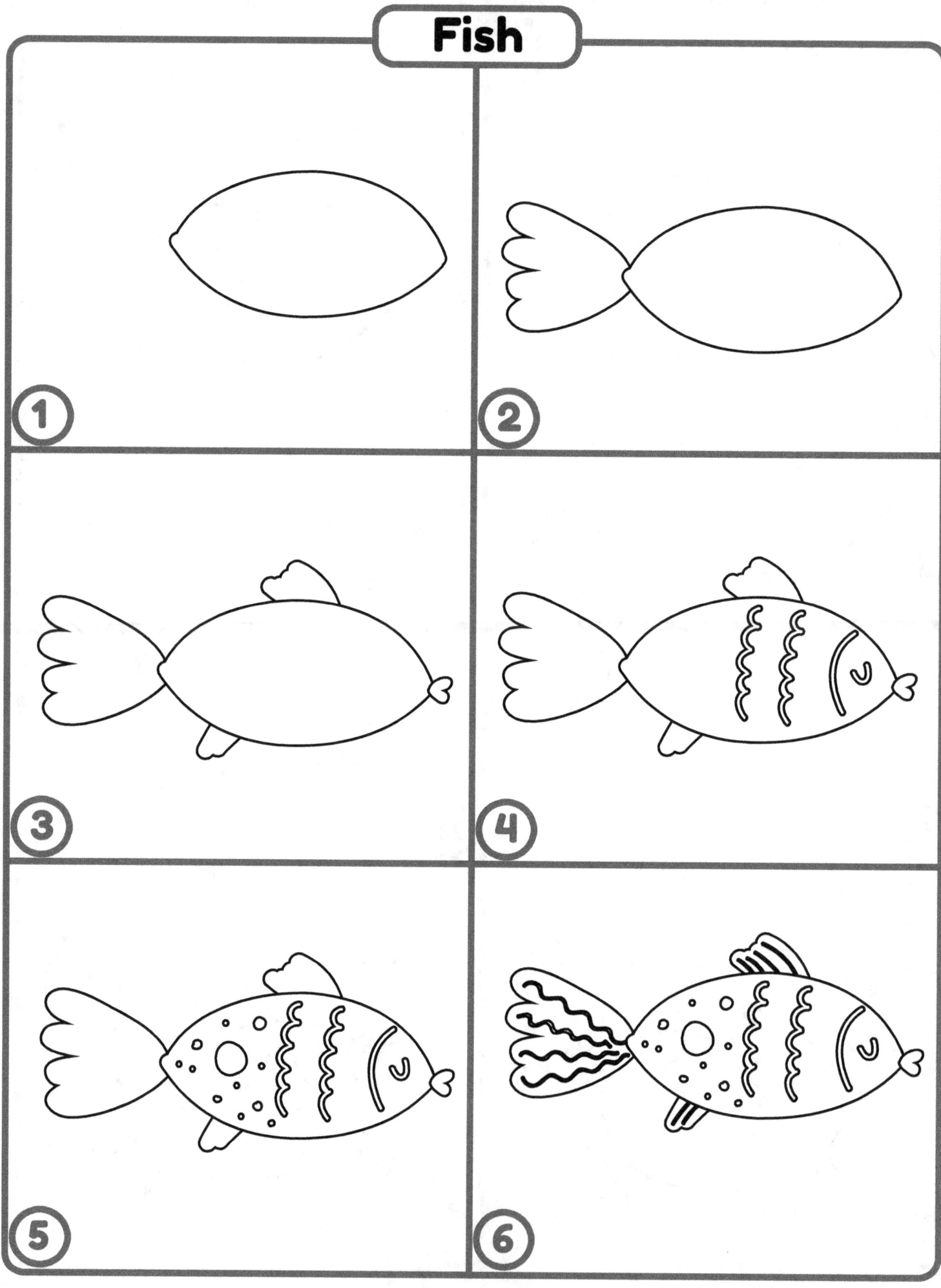

# Clams

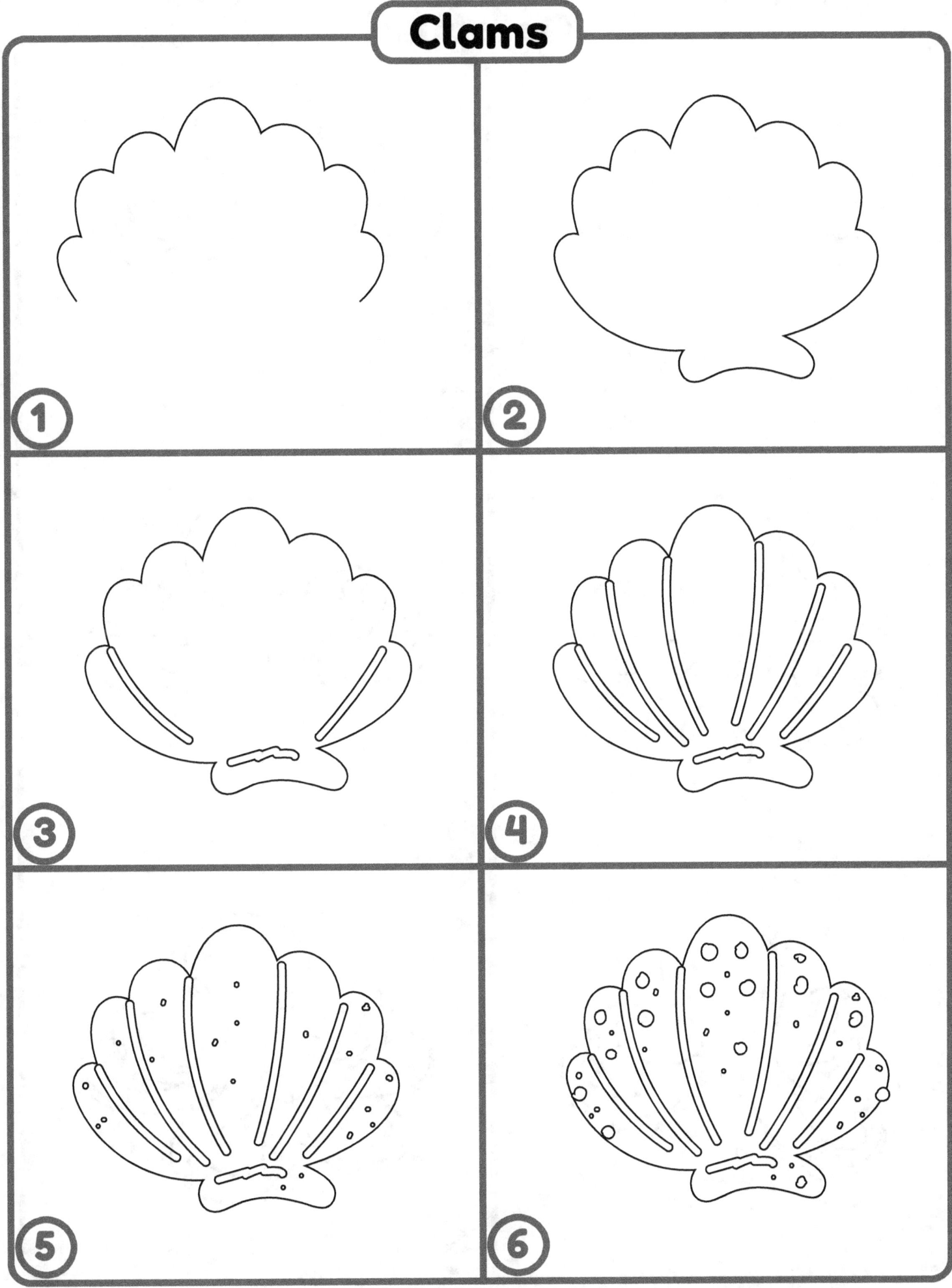

# Octopus

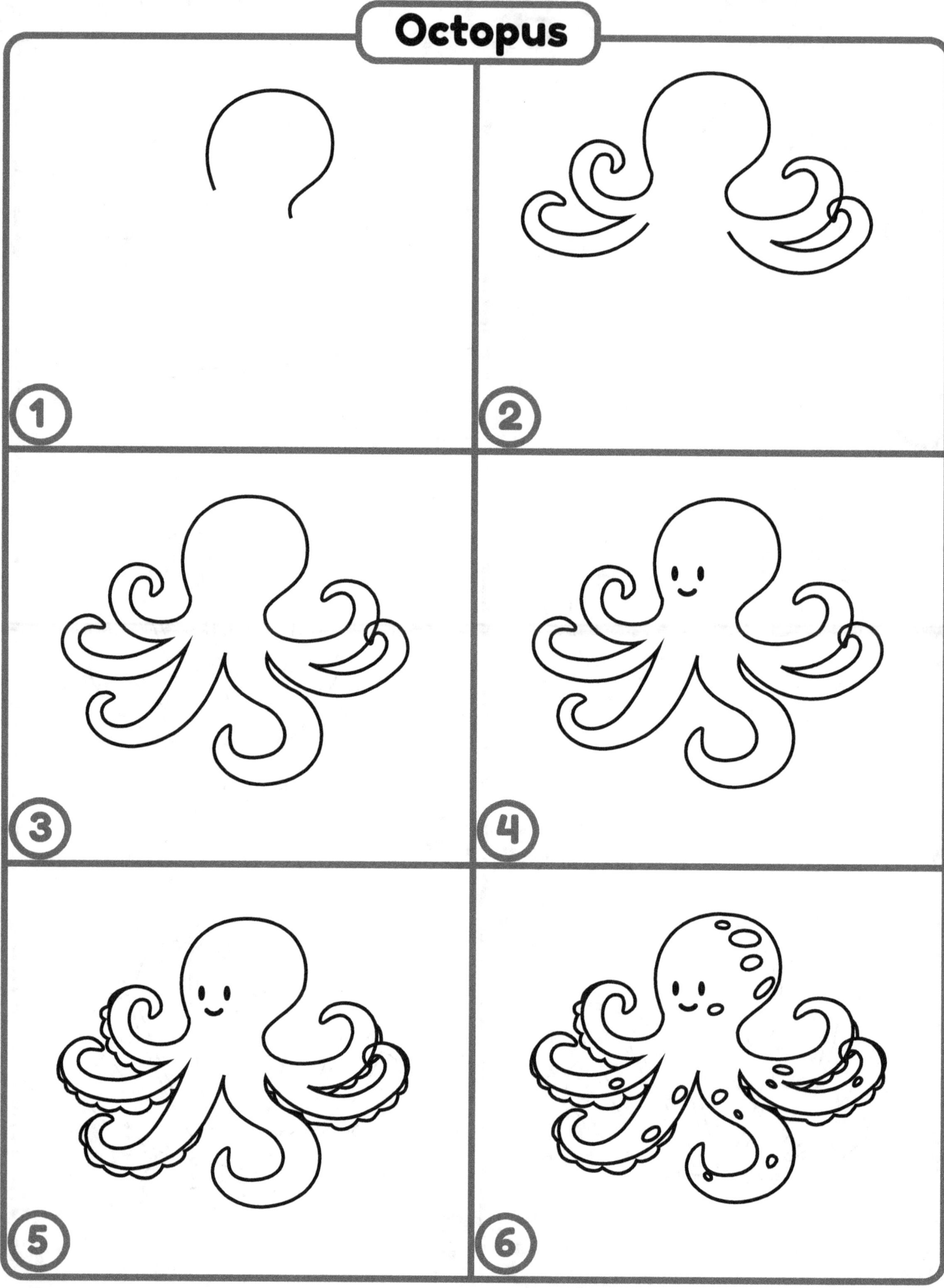

# Walrus

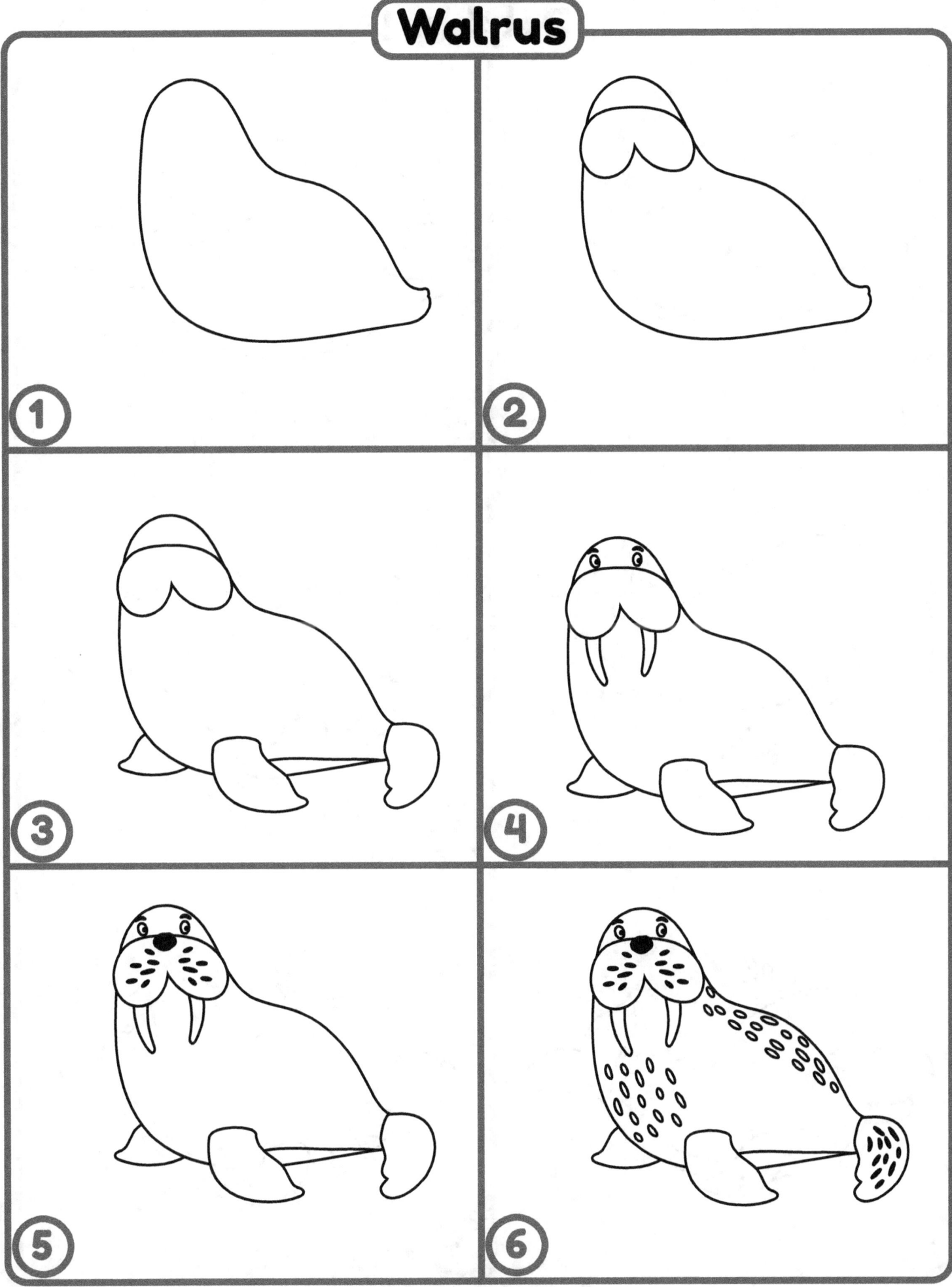

# Dolphin

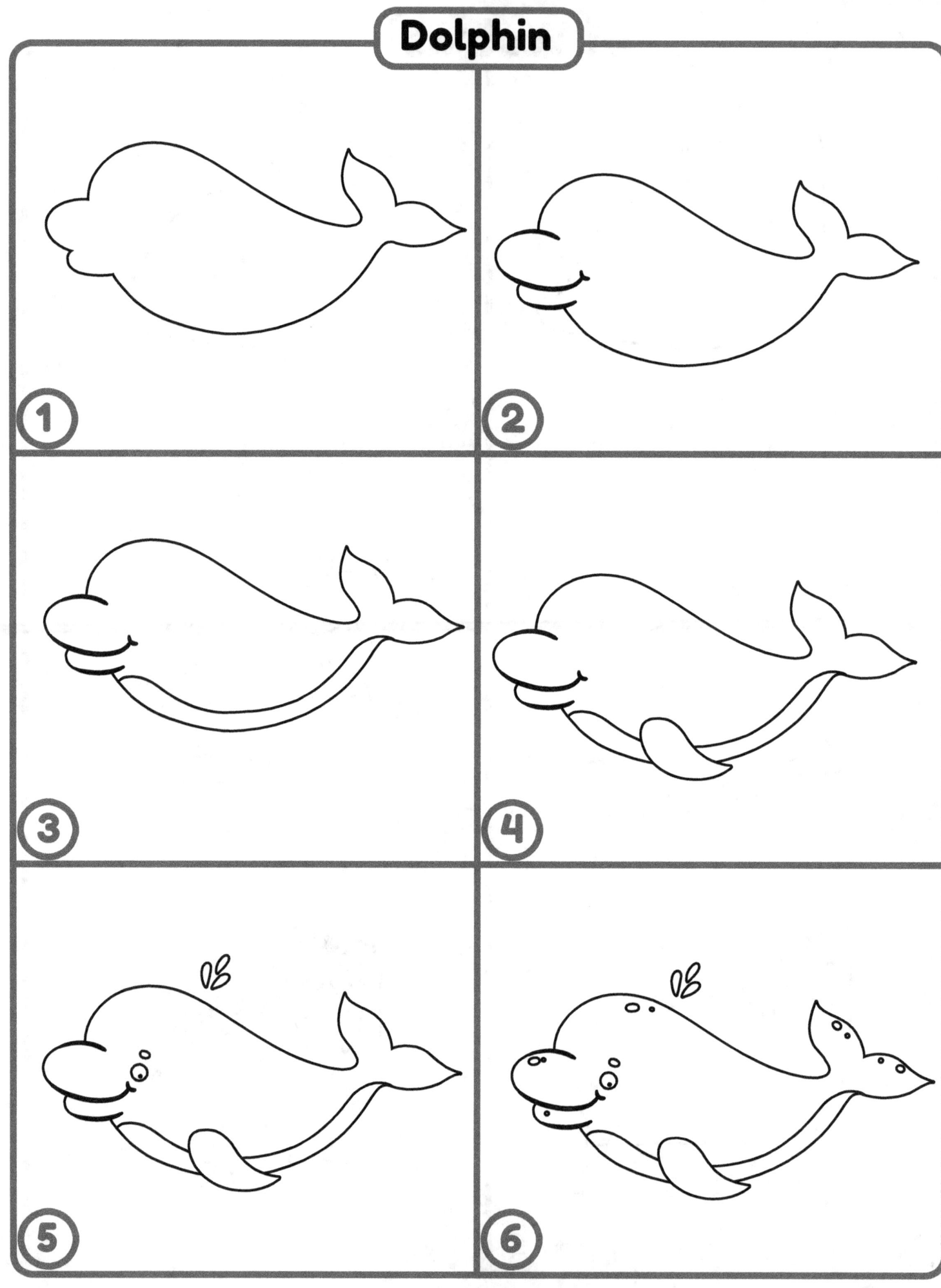

# Seal

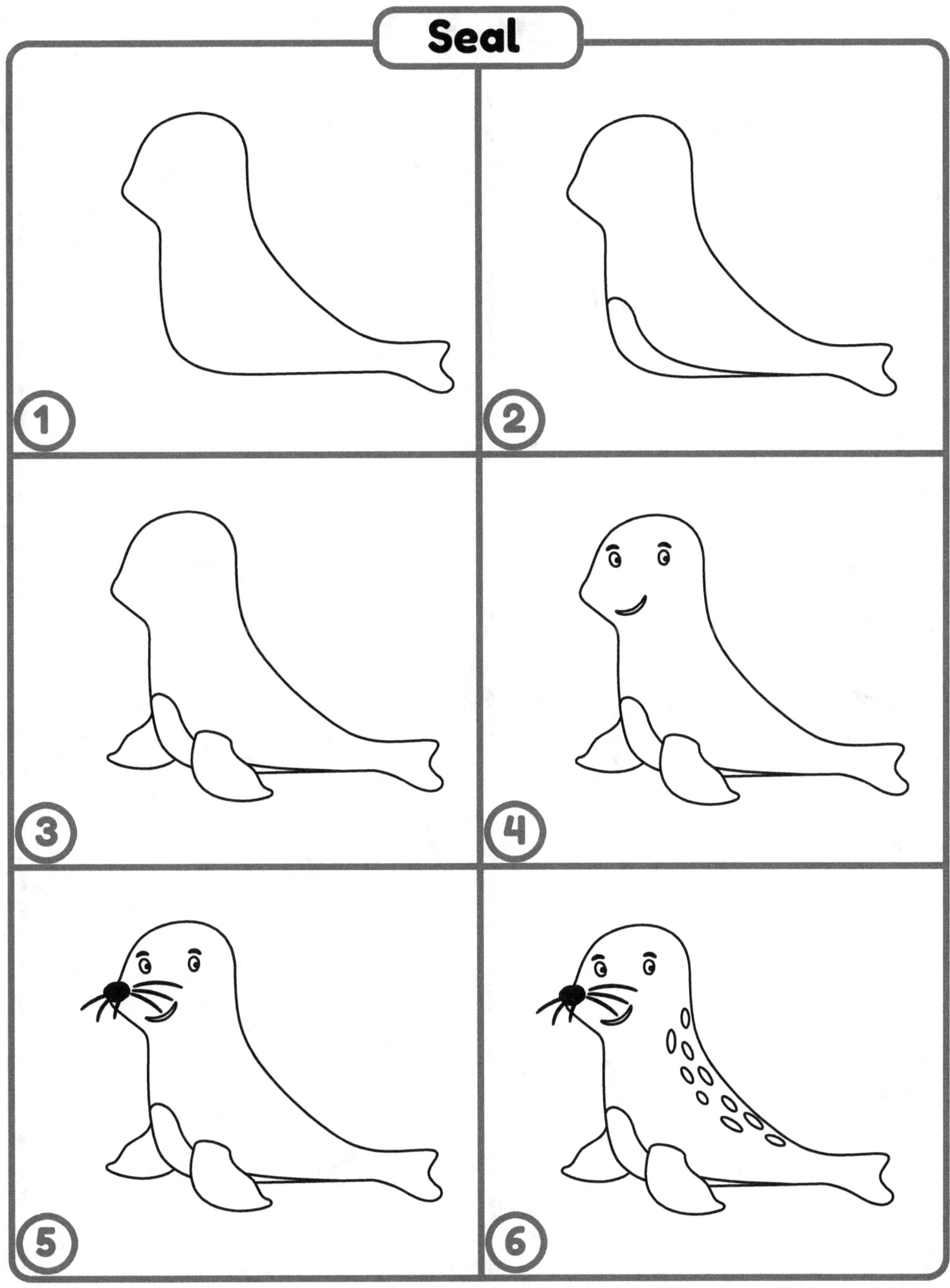

# Shark

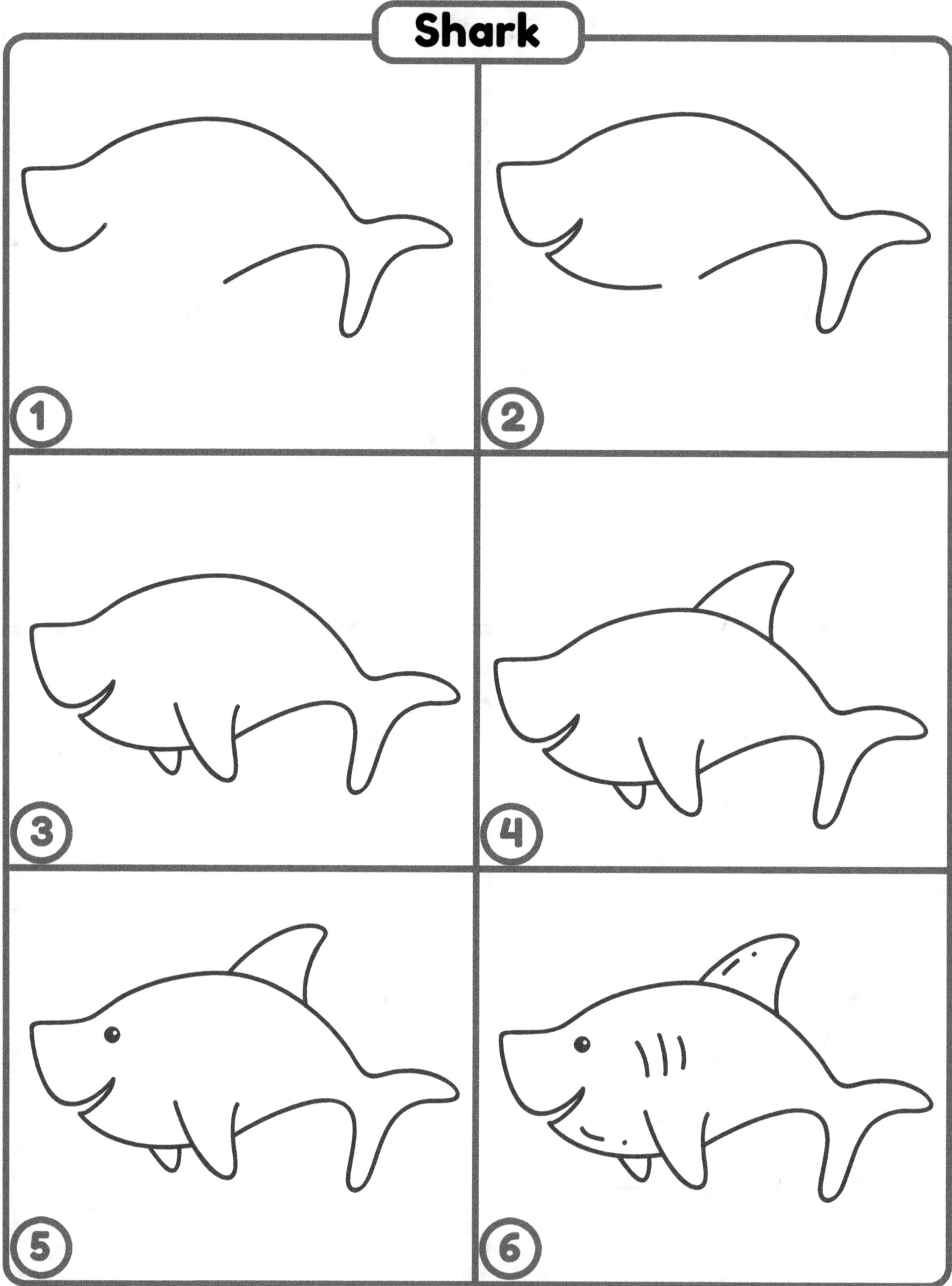

# Seahorse

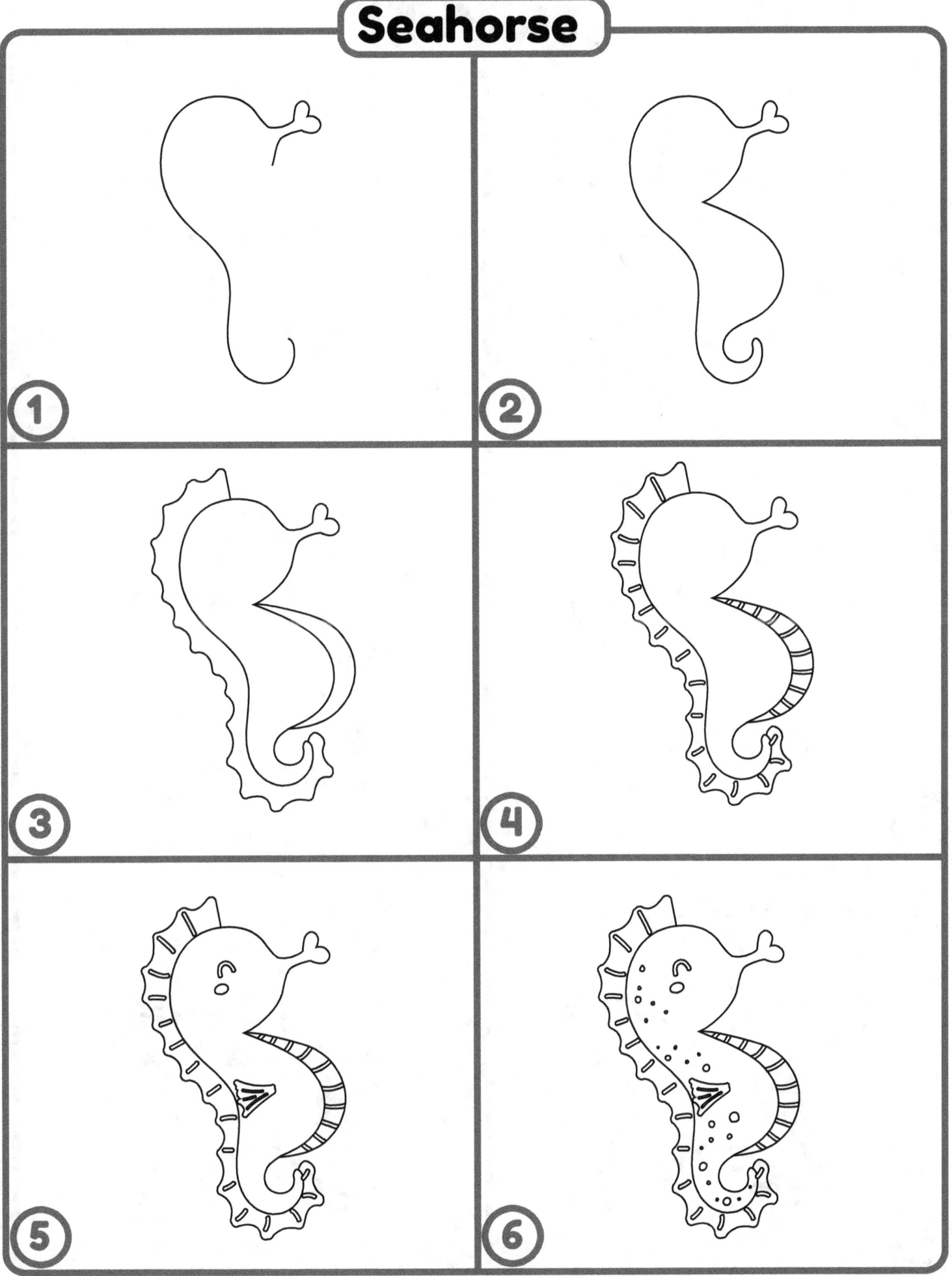

# Starfish

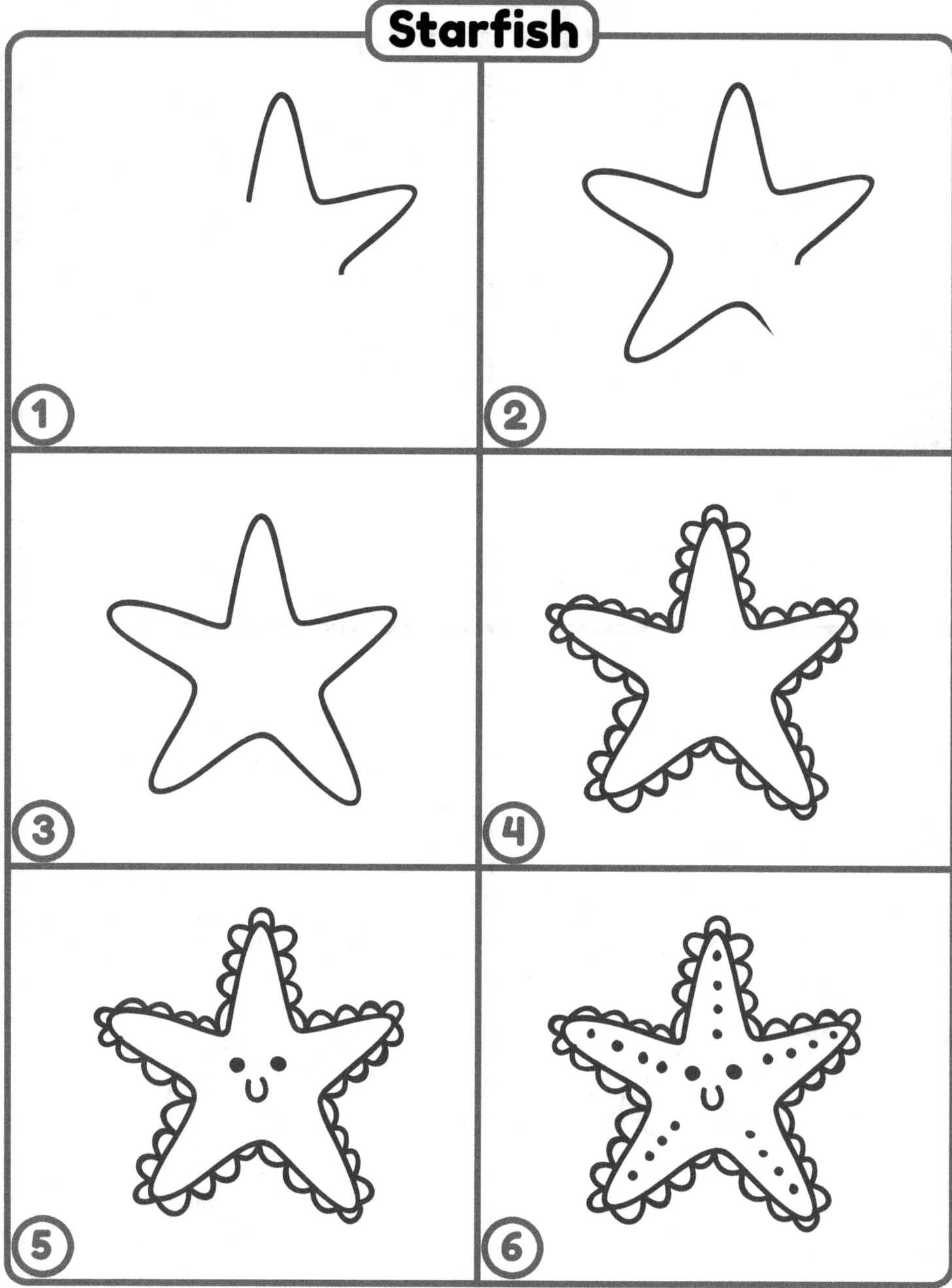

# Whale

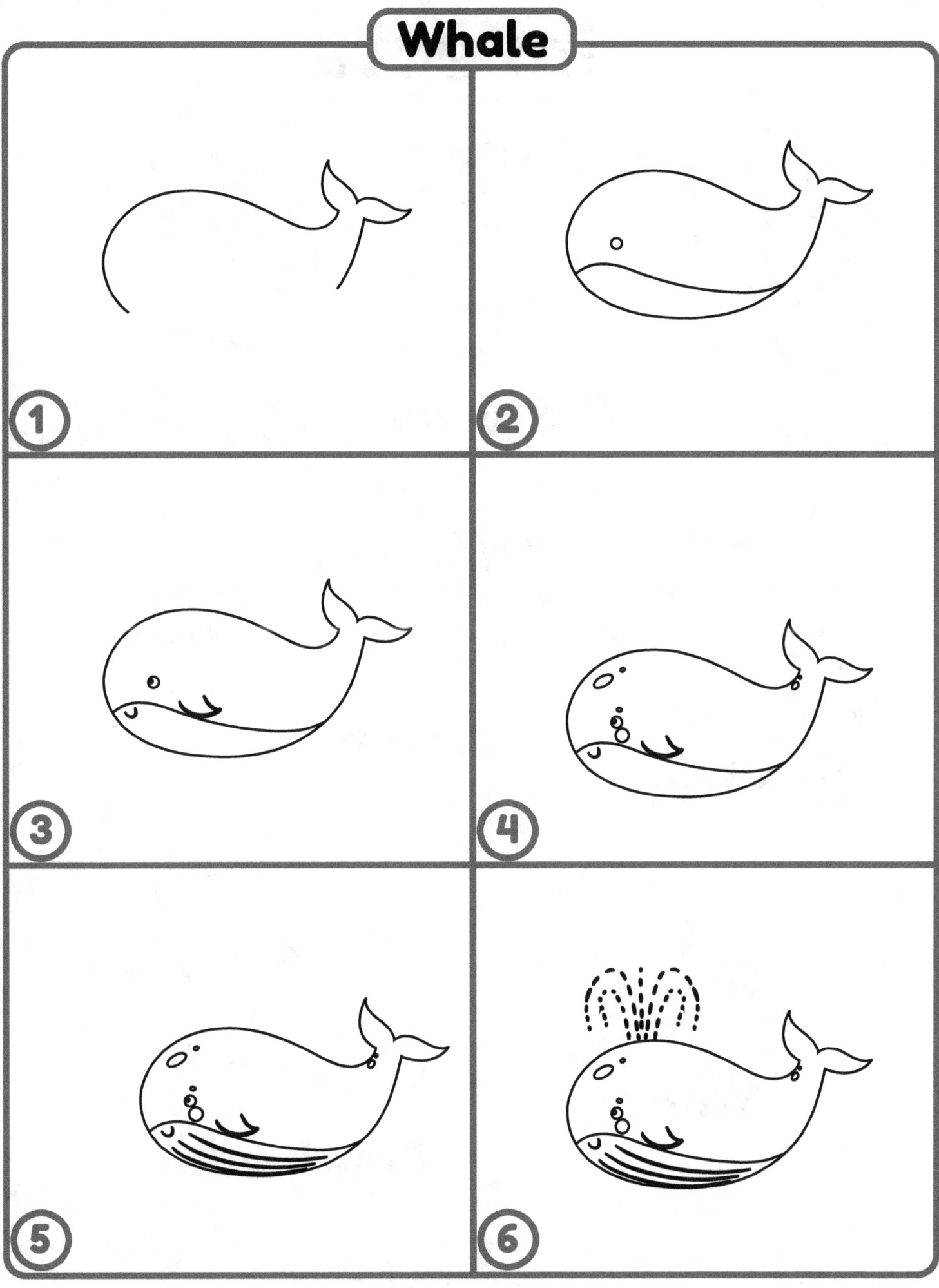

# Insects

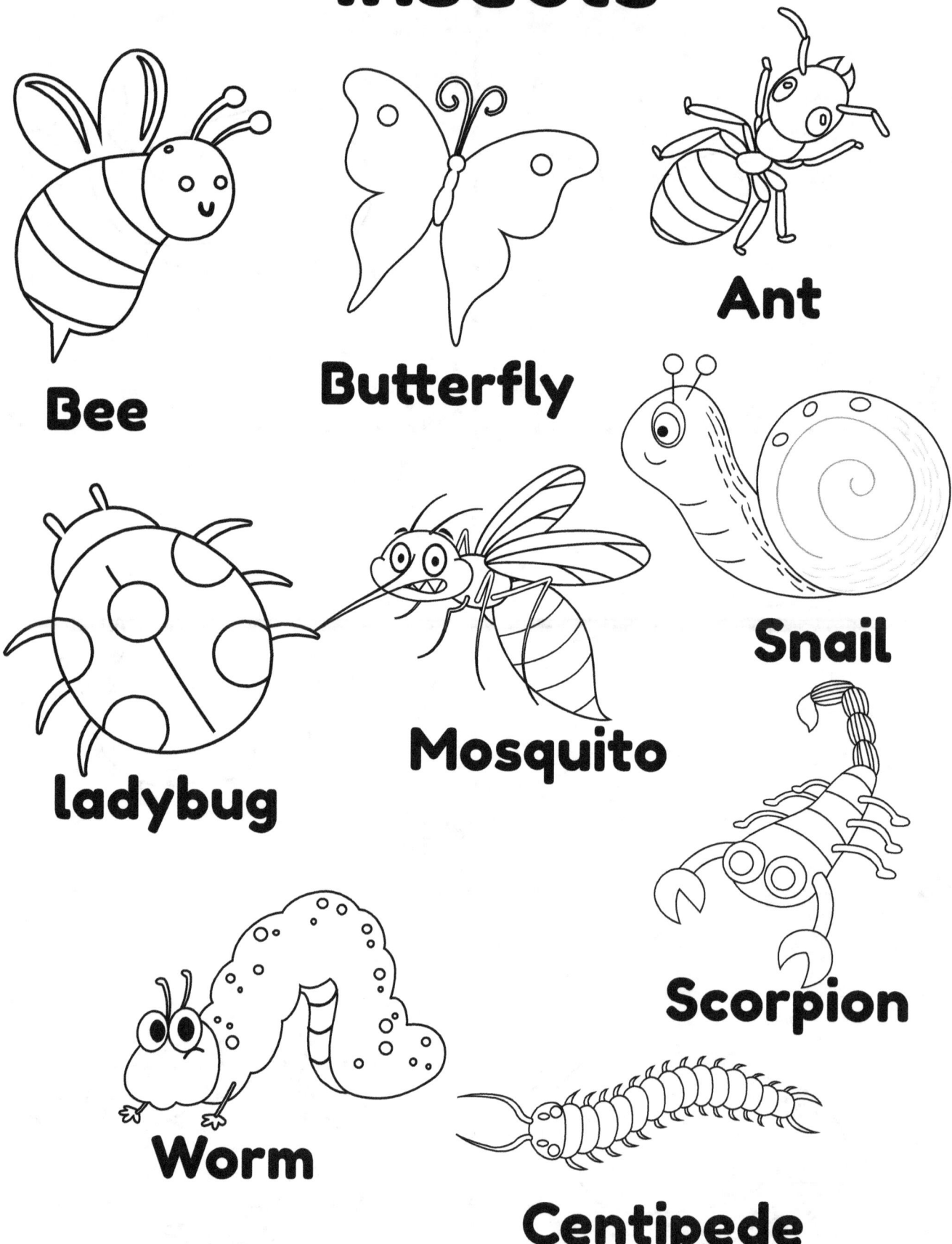

Bee

Butterfly

Ant

Snail

ladybug

Mosquito

Scorpion

Worm

Centipede

# Bee

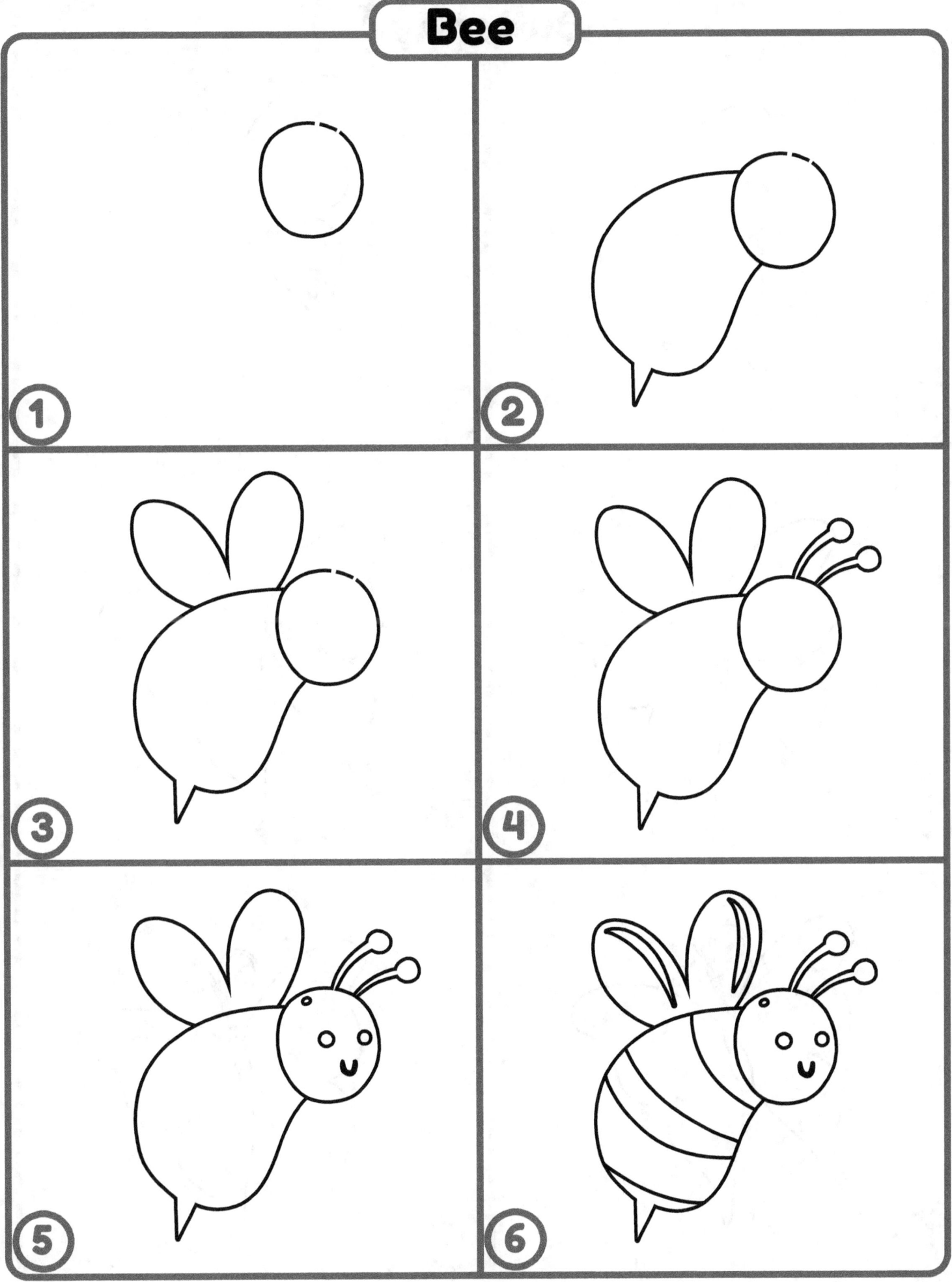

# Butterfly

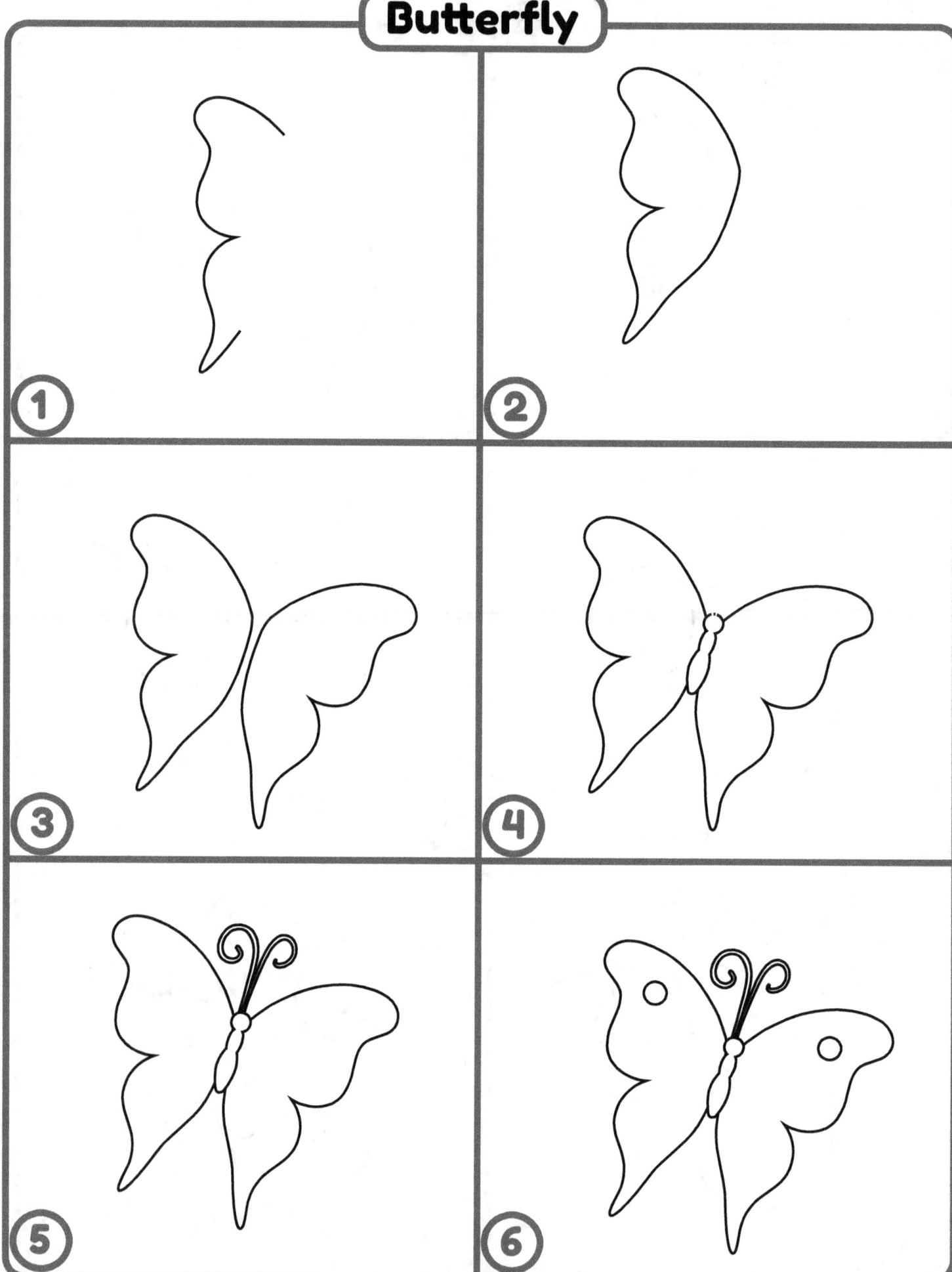

# Scorpion

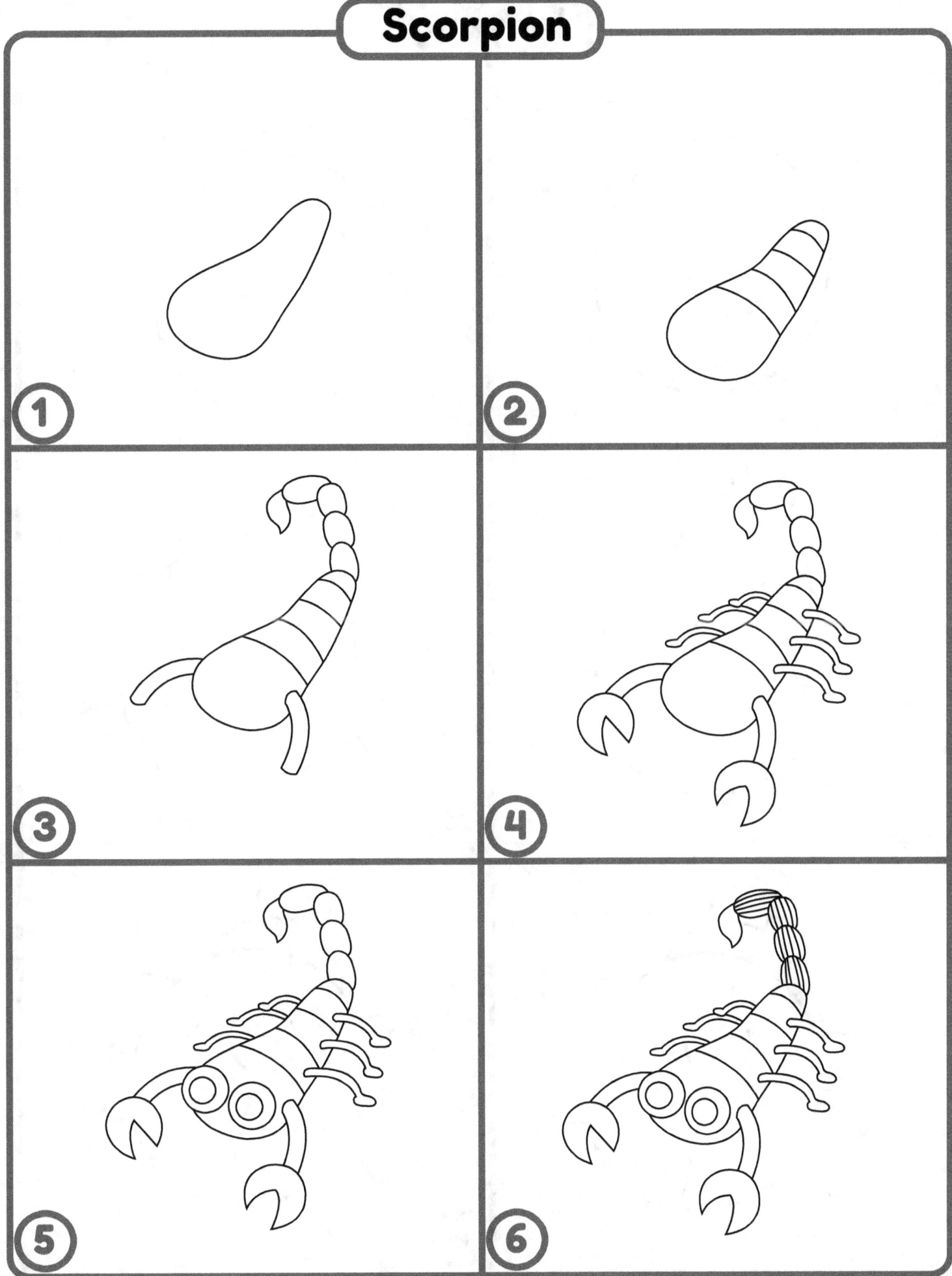

# ladybug

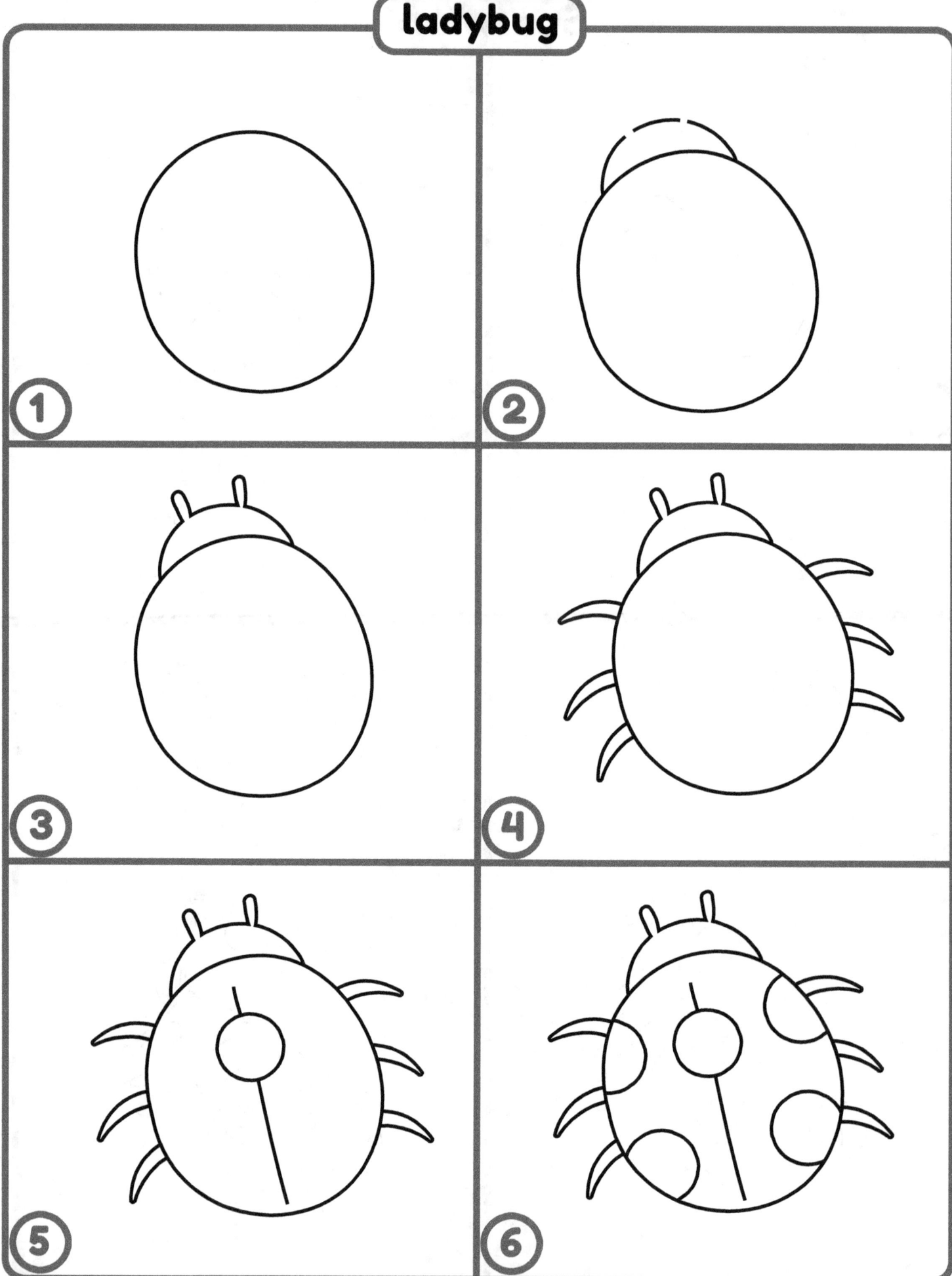

# Ant

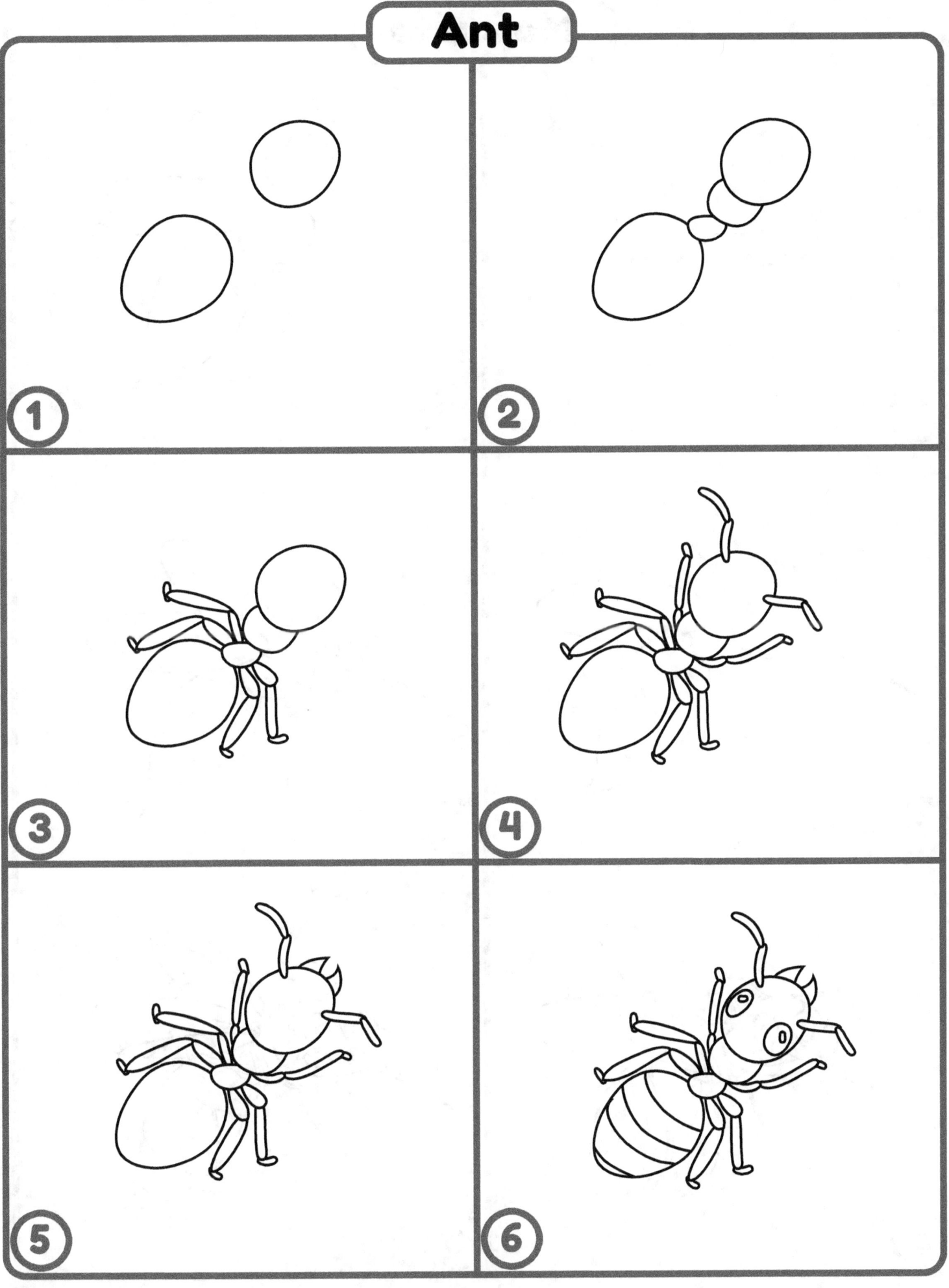

# Mosquito

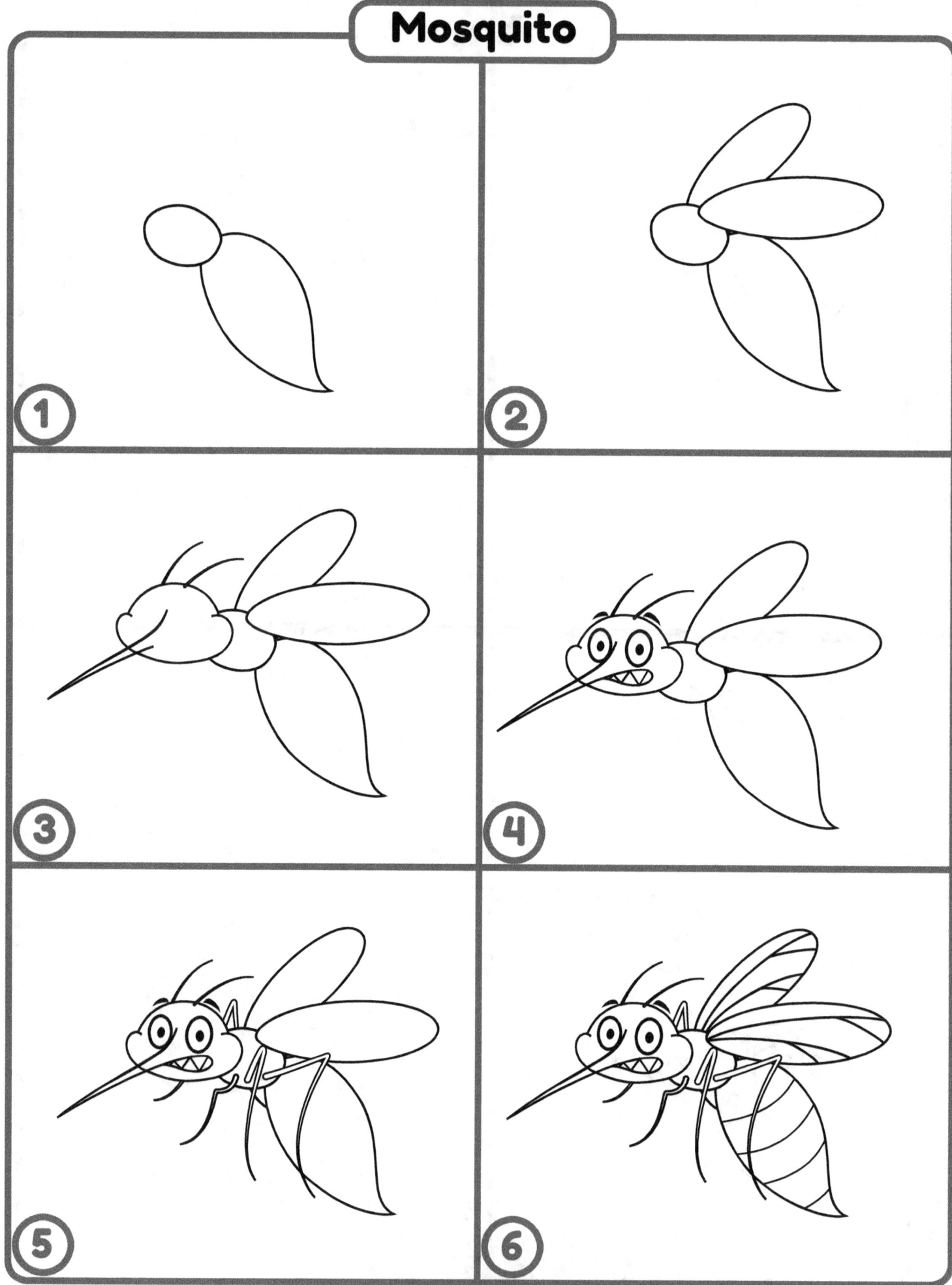

# Snail

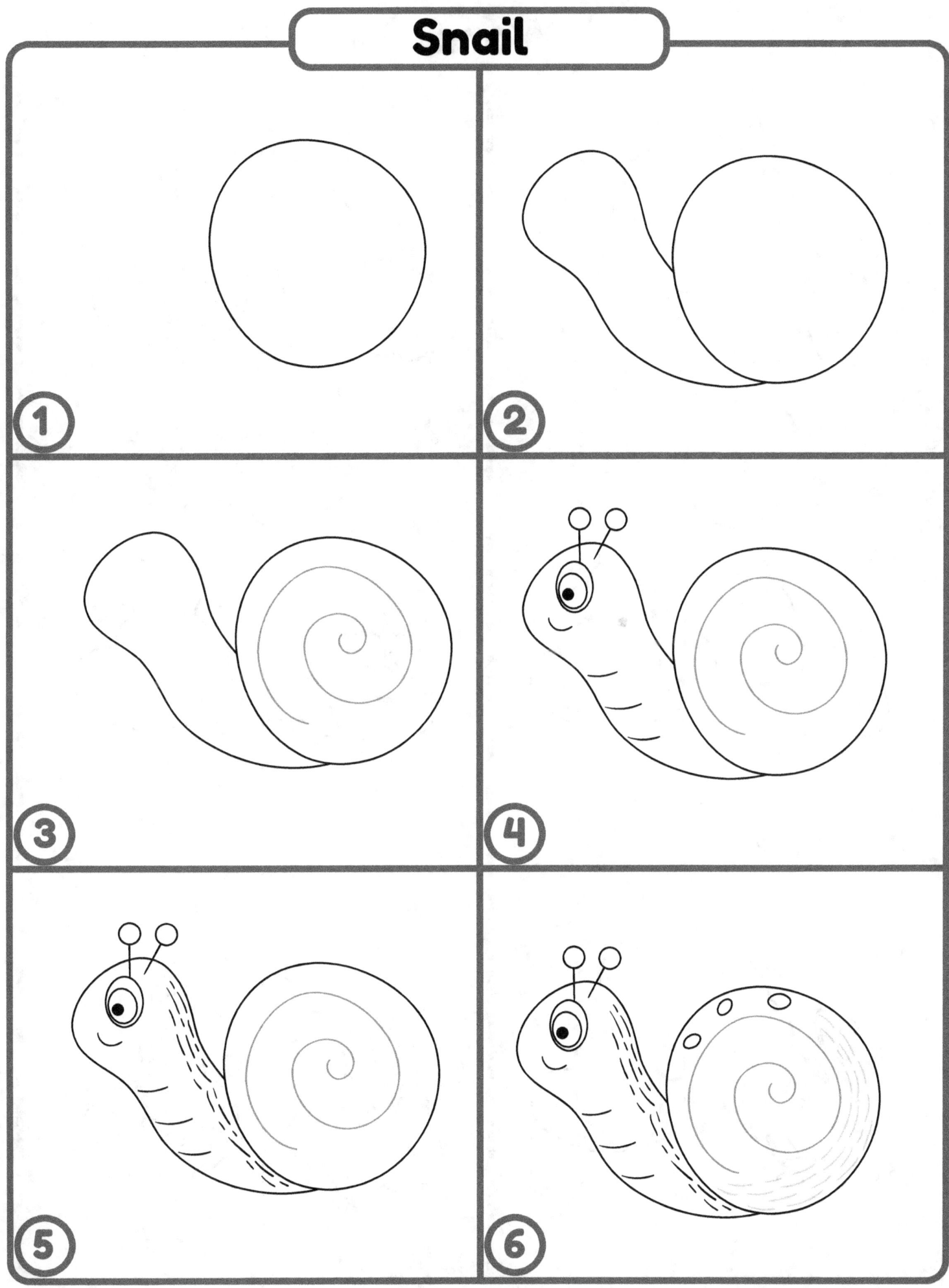

# Worm

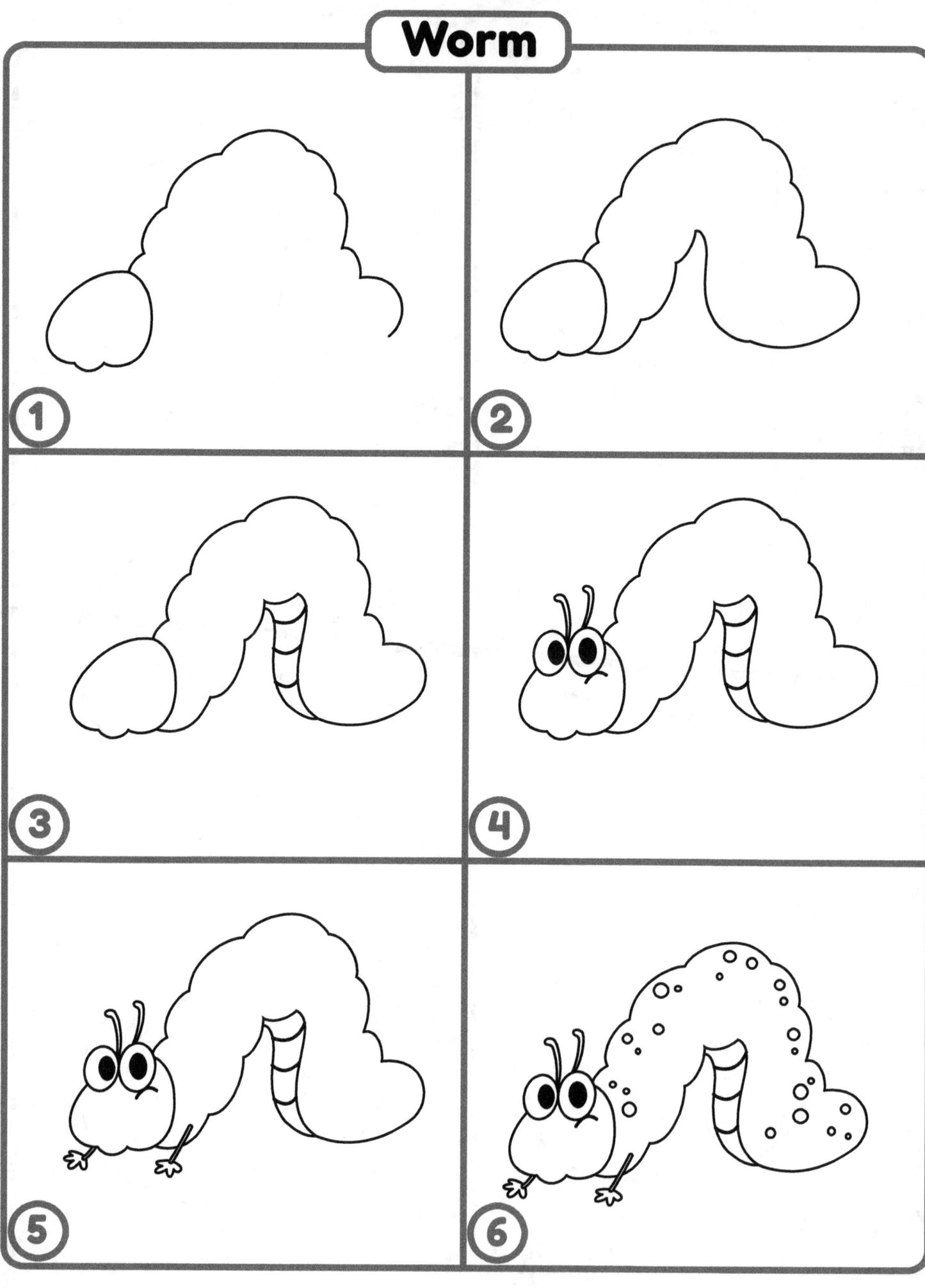